A BILLION LIES

The Highest Ranks of the Church Couldn't Throw Him Out Fast Enough

RYAN PRESCOTT

TABLE OF CONTENTS

INTRODUCTION

The purpose of this work is to provide you with a different view on Mike Rinder, the one he desperately tries to bury.

When Rinder was in the Church of Scientology, he was not considered as someone who had "authority", he was seen as a disrespectful person with a major self-importance problem.

What you are going to learn about are matters Rinder has intentionally kept from you and has labeled as "false" because it goes against the narrative that he is trying to push onto you. This narrative is blatant lies.

He is on a campaign to spread false information about Scientology to "get back" at David Miscavige, the ecclesiastical leader of the religion, for expelling him after the leader discovered all his breaches to common sensical policies and his resistance to using any policy or directive of the Church.

Rinder was a nightmare to work with and the highest ranks of the Church threw him out.

BILLION YEAR PLEDGE

Here is an introduction to the title of the book and why it was worded in this way. I will be telling you about a commitment to Scientology's religious order and Mike Rinder's attempt at spreading as many lies as possible about his former religion – which may end up numbering close to a billion. I have lost count. This comes from the many references to the billion figure.

Every great religion in history has at its core a group of people dedicated to helping the religion achieve its aims and on a massive scale. These people in Scientology are part of the *Sea Organization*, or commonly referred to as the Sea Org.

Members of the Sea Org may not number a lot (compared to the number of Scientologists internationally), but they are mighty and are in crucial roles in every aspect of the structure of Scientology. Their responsibilities are to keep the religion's technology pure and applied as intended through the writings of its Founder and forwarding the expansion of the religion without halting. You will only find a Sea Org member in the most crucial and trusted positions in the religion and that is primarily due to the amount of dedication that is required to ensure the duties in these positions are handled straight away and with full attention to the task at hand. Non-members are unable to provide this due to their obligations outside of the Church.

The Sea Org was formed in 1967 when L. Ron Hubbard retired from his position as the Executive Director International of the Church of

Scientology. He set to sea with a crew of veteran Scientologists to continue research into the advanced spiritual levels.

What happened from this moment brought forward what is referred to as the "billion-year pledge" and this is a show of commitment to the aims of Scientology through the application of the Church's belief that Man is a spiritual being and is not his mind or body and that he has lived other lives than this one. The billion-year pledge was formed by these veteran Scientologists to signify their devotion to the religion as immortal spiritual beings.

Frank K. Flinn, Ph.D., Adjunct Professor in Religious Studies stated this after his research into Scientology's religious order and this pledge:

"The Sea Organization, or "Sea Org," of the Church of Scientology had its genesis among the small group of Scientologists who accompanied Scientology's Founder, L. Ron Hubbard (1911–1986), on his extended sea voyages beginning in 1967. It was during these voyages that Mr. Hubbard undertook to develop the spiritual advanced Operating Thetan (OT) levels of the auditing process. These deeply dedicated Scientologists who witnessed Mr. Hubbard religious labors formed the Sea Organization by taking vows of service for a billion years in order to signify their commitment to the Church of Scientology and its mission. The billion-year vow of the Sea Organization member parallels almost exactly the Vow of Infinite Compassion of the one who undertakes to become a Bodhisattva in Mahayana Buddhism: "The Bodhisattva resolves: I take upon myself the burden of all suffering ... I must rescue all these [sentient] beings from the stream of Samsara [cycle of rebirth resulting from performing bad deeds]... I am resolved to abide in each state of woe for numberless aeons; and so I will help all

beings to freedom, in all states of woe that may be found in any world system whatsoever." Quoted from Edward Conze, ed., Buddhist Texts through the Ages (New York: Harper & Row, 1954), p. 131."

It is a misconception that those who are Scientologists (and not members of the Sea Org) sign this pledge to become a member of the Church of Scientology. **Becoming a Scientologist does not include you signing this pledge.**

In the religious order, Scientologists are introduced to the basics of taking care of themselves and presenting themselves as professionals both by appearance and by skill. The Church officials make sure each member has all their questions answered, that each member knows where to find necessities as a member and is started on the training for their entrusted position. The entry into the religious order is particularly designed to increase their confidence, their ability to work as a team to achieve a result, and their competence in their future position.

Common with other religions, Scientology ensures the information on other services are not administered to those who are not done with the previous service. The services in Scientology are to be done in proper order to achieve the intended result after each service (in Scientology counseling there is an intended result for the person. i.e., the ability to communicate on any subject and without considerations), therefore the Sea Org members are in-charge of ensuring the correct delivery of the higher-level services. It could confuse a person and cause the person to spend many more hours on the services to get through the misunderstandings he had of doing the higher-level services without doing the prerequisites.

You will find Sea Org members in Churches throughout the world handling positions that are only entrusted to them, operating the Church's advanced locations (which are responsible for the delivery of the higher spiritual services), the religion's and Church's management organizations

(Religious Technology Center, Church of Scientology International) and the facilities in place to disseminate and make Scientology materials available to all (Bridge Publications, Church of Scientology International Dissemination and Distribution Center and New Era Publications in Denmark, home of the Scientology Network - Scientology Media Productions, and the film production studio - Golden Era Productions).

In Scientology there are scriptures that are available to those who have achieved certain spiritual awareness levels and are ready to receive this information and move forward in their awareness. This scripture is entrusted to members of the Sea Organization to administer to Scientologists in advanced Churches of Scientology, which can be referred to as Advanced Organizations.

What a member can expect in exchange for their dedication to the religion is housing, meals, uniforms, medical and dental care. They are also given free Scientology training and auditing (spiritual counseling) to improve their mental and spiritual wellness, as their physical needs are being met with perfection.

There are those who do not make it in the Sea Org, meaning they are dismissed, or they simply would like to leave, and they go through a process to ensure any, and all questions are answered, upsets are resolved, items are returned to the Church, and tasks are turned over.

LITIGATION TROLL

"To believe the statements of this tiny handful of spiteful apostates, in the face of such overwhelming evidence to the contrary, would be to listen to the testimony of Judas Iscariot. Their lies are no less bold, baldfaced or malicious."
Mike Rinder, Affidavit

Mike Rinder and his litigation game is exposing his blatant disrespect for the legal system. He wastes the court's time with lies to force the Church of Scientology to settle using parishioner donations.

"Though they either do not know David Miscavige, or had some remote contact with him many years ago, they are willing to make vindictive allegations, not based on personal knowledge or the truth, and defame him personally and as the leader of the religion. The tactic is as transparent as it is unconscionable – spread venom in the hope that the victims of the hate campaign will eventually be forced to buy their silence so the Church can get on with its real purpose of expanding the Scientology religion and helping more people."
Mike Rinder, Affidavit

Rinder aims to make an unbelievable amount of money from painting Scientology what it is not by using these legal papers for publicity stunts (even though the cases in themselves have gone nowhere).

One of the people that used this system to go after the Church stated this:

"The fundamental premise upon which the Church's adversaries and their lawyers operate is the likelihood that courts and juries are willing to believe any allegation made against the Church by a former member, without regard to plausibility, contrary evidence, or the true facts. That concept was most succinctly expressed, on videotape, by anti-Scientology litigant, Gerald Armstrong, when he stated that a lack of documents or evidence was no impediment to litigating against the Church when the litigant can "just allege it."

The active pursuit of that litigation approach has now led to the formation of a small group of disaffected Scientologists who are now employed by an even smaller number of attorneys who are making a practice of litigating against the Church. This stable of witnesses can be relied upon to furnish "corroboration" for any allegation which an attorney wishes to make against the Church in pleadings at deposition, in affidavits, and ultimately in trial testimony."

Vicki Aznaran, Affidavit

Rinder is using the scam mentioned above to go after the Church for things they did not do. It does not even matter if one has witnessed something about the Church, Rinder will hire non witnesses to get them to corroborate stories from a group from the rabid anti-Scientology club.

"From 1972 until 1987, I was a member of various Church of Scientology ("Church") entities. During that time, I held a number of important positions in the corporate and ecclesiastical hierarchy of the Church. I was also a devout believer in the

religion of Scientology. In March of 1987, my husband Richard Aznaran and I left our positions with the Church and returned home to Texas from California. At the time we left, Richard and I voluntarily executed certain releases and waivers in full settlement of any and all disputes we had with the Church. In April of 1988, notwithstanding our execution of those releases and waivers, Richard and I filed a lawsuit against several Church entities and individuals in the United States District Court for the Central District of California.

"During the time I was a senior Church executive, I gained firsthand knowledge of the manner in which some apostate former Church members had pursued civil claims against the Church, and obtained successful verdicts or judgments or favorable settlements notwithstanding the merits. The courts consistently allowed the Church's adversaries leeway to introduce allegations without regard to the normal rules of procedure and evidence. At the time, this was a source of great concern to me, both as a Scientologist and a Church executive, particularly since my staff duties included responsibilities regarding certain areas of litigation.

"Thus, having participated in Scientology litigation both as a Church executive and as a litigant against the Church, I bring two distinct, but related, perspectives to this declaration from my personal knowledge and observation. First, at the time my husband and I brought our own suit I understood that the legal system could be used to pursue my position. Later, upon having sued various Scientology churches and having allied myself with other litigants and their counsel suing Scientology churches, I observed first hand the ways in which the legal system is

successfully used by litigants and counsel opposing the Church."
Vicki Aznaran, Affidavit

The courts do not always listen to cases having to do with information that is obviously geared towards the purpose of exploiting the Church for parishioner donations, the judge realizes what is happening through the evidence of the tactics tried by Rinder and his cohorts. That is exactly what happened with a case recently. The cases are being thrown to arbitration because these cases are nothing but attempts at getting money from their former religion, there is no factual basis for it.

For the last forty years, apostates have used the following against the Church to gain publicity, false "credibility" and money:

"The abusive device most consistently utilized by litigants and counsel adverse to the Church occurs in connection with the filing of declarations or affidavits. It is common knowledge among the stable of disaffected ex-Scientologists who supply such sworn statements that the attorneys dictate the desired content of such testimony with the primary, often sole, purpose of presenting inflammatory accusations that prejudice the Church in the eyes of the court. In such declarations or affidavits, context, the truth, and relevance to the issues in the case are disregarded altogether. As time has passed and this technique has evolved, anti-Church litigants and their counsel have become more and more emboldened in making such declarations and affidavits because the tactic has proven to be so effective in poisoning courts and juries against the Church."
Vicki Aznaran, Affidavit

This is how Rinder does it, he uses his cohorts in the anti-Scientology club and formulates exactly what he is going to "go after" Scientology for, starts a publicity campaign around it and then files it in court. He knows it will be thrown out nowadays and he can still use the publicity to scrounge up some more money from his small group of followers.

"There are other things I have seen and experienced in anti-Scientology litigation that seem very unusual to me. There is a group or "team" of anti-Scientology witnesses who are being paid for their testimony, and based on my experience, this testimony is being altered and falsified, either by the witnesses themselves or the attorneys. For example, Graham Berry, counsel of record for a defendant in the case of CSI V. FISHMAN, filed numerous declarations from ex-Scientologists after the lawsuit was dismissed which had been purchased for many thousands of dollars. Mr. Berry told me that these payments were made possible because his client had insurance coverage.

"In February of 1994, Mr. Berry called my husband and me and offered to hire us at the rate of $125 per hour for us to study materials in the FISHMAN case and to write declarations supporting issues Mr. Berry wished us to support in the FISHMAN case. Mr. Berry gave us an advance of $2,500, which we were expected to bill against services rendered. He told us that because his client in the FISHMAN case had insurance coverage, the insurance money enabled him to do this. He said he was able to get the insurance company to pay our salaries by naming us as "experts", which also enabled the use ((of)) our declarations without regard to whether we were actually witnesses to the events at issue in the FISHMAN case, which we were not.

"Mr. Berry told us he had assembled a team of former Scientologists for use in litigation, all of whom were employed by him in the FISHMAN case as so-called experts. Although we were

not eager to get involved in FISHMAN's litigation, we agreed to do (so) because the $2,500 advance by Mr. Berry was attractive. Mr. Berry sent us some documents from the court record in the FISHMAN case, which I read, since I was being paid $125 per hour to do so."

Vicki Aznaran, Affidavit

Most of the time, anti-Scientology clan will try to pull out allegations which cannot be countered, in which case the Church ensures the court knows it is not true and requests the court to request more evidence. The anti-Scientology clan hates this move so they revert to getting the media talking about it so they can get the court riled up to rule a certain way, most likely in favor of the anti-Scientology clan.

"In June 1998 I was featured in a forty-minute segment on Dateline ... The program focused on my activities concerning Scientology. Throughout the filming of the Dateline program, Mr. Dandar indicated his excitement at the possibility of more sensational anti-Scientology coverage on national television, especially if I could get Dateline to focus on the ... case. Mr. Dandar told me he was anxious to have any media against Scientology especially if it would have some impact on the jury pool in Florida.

"Mr. Dandar encouraged me to get as much negative media about Scientology as possible and I gave media interviews whenever I could. I attended and organized regular picketing of Scientology facilities - which Mr. Dandar and others in the trial team also attended on occasion. ..."

Robert Minton, Affidavit

Additional to Vicki's statements through affidavit, there was an investment banker by the name of Robert Minton. He was the anti-Scientology clan's major investor for attacks against Scientology, especially in relation to a witch hunt in Clearwater, Florida. He stated the above in an affidavit, after he found out the harsh truth that he was just being used for his money and that he was drawn into an illegal operation and that he helped in attempts at swinging court decisions in the way he would benefit by utilizing willing media outlets.

How are people able to do this? How are Rinder's cohorts able to get away with this?

Blatantly trying to persuade a jury, through media especially, makes this a witch hunt against Scientology, or anything you are suing. If there was actual evidence that supported your allegations, you would not need to put over a million dollars into publicity to force the jury to vote a certain way. In fact, you would just let the case go through and respect the outcome. This does not happen when you have the intention of stealing parishioner donations from your former religion.

Further evidence that these cases and claims are completely witch hunts would be the following statement from Minton:

"...I told Mr. Dandar that we really wanted him to focus the case on Scientology and its leadership ... It is my belief that because I was funding the case, and in order to ensure that I would continue to do so, Mr. Dandar was willing to shift the emphasis of the case from a simple wrongful death suit to a case against the beliefs and practices of Scientology. At the end of this meeting, Mr. Dandar said this would cost more and I then handed Mr. Dandar a check for $250,000, bringing the total I had loaned ... at that time to $750,000. ...

"In the fall of 1999 I flew into the Tampa airport and was picked

up ... and taken to Mr. Dandar's new office ... in Tampa for a meeting considering whether Mr. Dandar should add David Miscavige as a defendant in the wrongful death case. ... The focus of the discussion was not what the facts were concerning Mr. Miscavige, but how to pressure him.

"Mr. Dandar was enthusiastic about this prospect even though there was no evidence to support it, as he felt it would force Scientology to the settlement table and would increase the amount of any settlement that Scientology would agree to. He also stated this would generate sensational publicity for the case. During the meeting, Dr. Garko (Mr. Dandar's trusted business partner) specifically pointed out that there was not a single shred of evidence to support adding Mr. Miscavige and was opposed to adding him as a defendant.

"The whole theory of adding Mr. Miscavige was based on an affidavit of Jesse Prince dated August 20, 1999, which I have reviewed and which has been filed in this case, speculating about events in December 1995, three years after Mr. Prince had left Scientology staff. This was the pattern used in this and other Scientology cases I have seen - an attorney comes up with a strategy and gets one of the paid "Scientology experts" to come up with a theory and write an affidavit that could be used to support a court filing based purely on speculation and written with allegations by innuendo."

Robert Minton, Affidavit

They invented these cases intending to go after Scientology. Somehow the courts were ignorant enough to accept them. What does that show you about any case against you? What would happen if someone when a U.S. court put a judgement against them, the foreign court refused to recognize it. The Church lost out on whatever money was left on the project.

"When I met with the owner I didn't do my homework, I re-negotiated the contract based on my 'personal ability' and that I could talk 'legal terms' better than the owner of the company."
Mike Rinder

In 2006, Mike Rinder admitted to these situations and more in a list that he titled "Damage I Have Caused". But, of course, knowing what Rinder does, the Church would find out about his felonies involving a case in Clearwater, Florida, that were exposed in 2009 by his cohort, Mark "Marty" Rathbun on the news. This was strategically exposed right after the statute of limitations expired.

Rinder has admitted that he has "avoided responsibility" and that he managed to avoid all consequences for his actions that caused disasters in his Scientology career.

"This was motivated by a cowardly desire to have 'someone other than me to blame' if the situation blows up."
Mike Rinder

Now you can see why the highest ranks in the Church of Scientology could not throw him out fast enough. He was a walking disaster in the Church.

What is the one reason some reporters disliked talking to Scientology? Mike Rinder and his "handling" of situations. He did not use Church policy and if he did the reporters would get their questions answered immediately and would invite them to tour the facilities they are interested in, provide interviews, and supply them with materials that would provide them with additional information.

The Church receives a lot of press about its beliefs, practices, new organizations, millions of members, etc. Rinder would know this due to the number of requests received from reporters internationally. It is overwhelming but the Church handles it correctly today and does this job very well (compared to a person who used zero Church policy and created upset everywhere he went).

For instance, a German news crew landed in Los Angeles to visit the Church of Scientology as they wanted to film some of the Church's activities for a segment they were going to do. In 1996, Germany was filled with those who opposed religion and especially Scientology, the news crew was just in town to cover some of the activities and go back to broadcast it. The Church itself was fully aware of this and there was nothing against it. The Church was appreciative that their activities were being shown even at a time where some in Germany were attacking religions, including Scientology.

But there was one person who did not approve and for whatever reason decided to "go after" these reporters with hostile confrontations, a car chase and hitting their car. This is what he called "media relations" and the Church would call them something entirely different – insanity.

Next was a magazine reporter who was asking questions to the Church and involving the Church in his piece. Rinder took this opportunity to challenge the reporter, intentionally irritating the reporter and giving terribly incomplete and trash answers to the reporter. In fact, when the reporter published the piece, it was nothing more than a pile of confusion. This is not what the Church does at all. Rinder wasted four days of the reporter's and the Church's time.

Rinder disliked Eastern Europe, so he decided to ignore a request from a magazine in that area and when reporters realized what was happening, they published a terrible cover story about the Church, thanks to Rinder's "views".

The last one came from a major newspaper who had requested information on a major story on the Church of Scientology and instead of handling it immediately, Rinder took three months to provide any sort of information and even return the call.

I am sure you see now why Rinder is no longer part of the Church of Scientology.

"Over the years…[I] created bigger and bigger disasters in my wake."

Mike Rinder

LIAR

"You know, as the old saying goes, if you lie about one thing then what's to say you didn't lie about everything else that you're saying?"

Mike Rinder

Mike Rinder lies. This is not new news. He lied in the Church of Scientology, and he lies outside it.

When you can admit in a deposition that you lie and that you lied to the leader of your former religion, you are going downhill in your life no matter what you think.

When you are faced with the truth about Rinder, you are also faced with the lies he spreads throughout the airwaves to counter the truth being stated about him. What Rinder speaks are lies and they are twisted to be believed and not given another thought. He says them and then puts another statement at the end to solidify it. It is a tactic he has always used, including to members to swindle them into believing his balderdash so that they could take the blame for Rinder's actions, and he would walk free of responsibility.

In fact, a lot of sane individuals are not believing Rinder because he has not provided proof about his false statements in over a decade. The sane observe the facts: he had numerous opportunities to handle it with the Church and did not, and he left his family and friends when he had all chances to stay with them. Why would anyone believe him when he states otherwise?

After all, even Rinder knows you are having second thoughts on his truthfulness, he knows you are onto him and so he stated this recently as a "middle ground" to give you a sense that he "cares":

> **"They [listeners] have got to make up their own mind. They've got to look at me. They've got to say, 'OK, what we see here is someone that we believe is telling the truth.' Or, 'What we see here is someone who seems to be just a liar.'"**
>
> Mike Rinder

A liar has a hard time owning up to what he has caused for himself and especially for others, so he tends to blame entities that are not involved simply because he knows people have not grasped a decent understanding of the entity – such as Scientology. He has tried to blame his lying onto the Church, and it brought me to this statement he made in a testimony:

> **"He says that telling lies...well, it's doomed to failure. It's a bad thing to do. It's sort of despicable....In fact, there are many other writings by Mr. Hubbard which conform with this concept of always telling the truth."**
>
> Mike Rinder, Affidavit

In Scientology, Rinder would "save his own neck" by lying to Church officials and even Mr. Miscavige about legal matters "being handled" when they were not and situations "completely handled" when they were not even being addressed. This obviously resulted in confusion in the Church's public and legal affairs and Mr. Miscavige was often pulled into these cycles to complete them.

After they were addressed, what did Rinder do? He blamed it on his juniors not doing their jobs and they would be removed from their positions or given a correction order to apply certain policies of the Church (when they were using these policies). The juniors gained a lot more knowledge and were able to handle even more after these correction orders.

Rinder testified that lying is frowned upon in the Church and is the cause of untrustworthiness surrounding people – Mr. Hubbard mentions a lot of information on this subject. Though Rinder continued to lie in the Church until he was removed from his position and any "executive" position he believed he was in and stripped of any "authority" he thought he had.

He wrote letters to Mr. Miscavige (not requested and not private) admitting his dishonesty, his "criminal moral code" and his "cowardice and lack of integrity". This admission was via a handwritten letter in 2003 (in the back of the book). This letter exposed the reasons why he lies and why he cannot tell the truth. These reasons still apply today.

Because of Mr. Miscavige's persistence over the years to help Rinder straighten his life out, Rinder even wrote a communication to Mr. Miscavige on this subject:

"I owe you something way beyond and in addition to an apology—my gratitude for saving my life. Your insistence, for months and years, that I get straight is the only thing that has actually brought me to my senses….I wasn't honest with myself, you or anyone else, as I continued to operate on a 'moral code' (justification) of what I could 'get away with.'"
Mike Rinder

So, for some reason Rinder wrote this communication and did not want to take any responsibility and *handle* the errors he made with the reporters, the legal cases and find out what he could do to assist the Church in repairing the damages he caused – two years later after not handling *anything* he was expelled from the Church.

Clearly, Rinder did not want to be a Scientologist any longer no matter what he said. He just could not take responsibility.

© Church of Scientology International – The historic Clearwater Bank Building. Now serving as the Scientology Public Information Center open to Scientologists from all around the world and the community.

These were the first two properties that started to fulfill the demand for Scientology at this stage of transitioning from a base on the ship to a base on land.

These were the first established locations for Scientology in this city and they were being renovated and prepared for the delivery of advanced services to the international congregation.

Since the acquiring of these two buildings, the Church has expanded into over forty buildings. In the process of this expansion, the Church has brought a lot to Clearwater. The Church has brought *thousands* to this city which has helped the local businesses, festivals, community organizations, tourism, and taxes back to the city.

As a religious organization, this would have been celebrated as incredible in sane societies.

On top of operating these properties for their parishioners, tours to the community and even a place to hunker down in times of natural disasters, the Church pays the city property taxes, tourist taxes, and even contributes to the community every week through volunteerism and even through their members and their contributions to citywide, statewide, and nationwide programs and organizations that help make change that is desperately needed. They have become a stable source of help for the community.

City of Clearwater

I do believe this aspect needs to be explained in detail. There have been attempts at silencing the Church from saying anything by those who hate religion and their meddling in this community.

Let us get the straight information from the beginning of Scientology in Clearwater.

I will warn you in advance, I will not be using tabloid tactics like you are used to getting from Rinder and the anti-Scientology clan.

In the 1970s, the Church needed an official location for their spiritual headquarters. The ship they were using before was found to be too small for the congregation, the management of the expanding religion, and the operating staff of the ship.

In 1975, the Church officially chose Clearwater, Florida. The Church then hired a buyer to ensure the Church got the best price, stayed within the budget, and ensured everything went as expected.

This is a normal procedure for real estate professionals. You will not find the Pope purchasing a property for his faith. You will find trusted buyers are necessary to save time and get what was intended without the price gouging and the added time for unnecessary special treatment.

After the purchase of the Fort Harrison Hotel and the Clearwater Bank Building, the Church moved towards repairs, preparations, and started the plans for the delivery of these advanced spiritual services.

As the city was found mostly abandoned and in need of a community – the Church was genuinely curious about the plans, the current scene, and meet the officials to build a relationship. The Church wanted to help get the community back on its feet since they were going to be part of it.

But, the City of Clearwater had something else planned.

The mayor at the time, Gabe Cazares, had ties to corrupt individuals. The abandonment, the damages, and the lack of community were all in the plans to the City of Clearwater as it was planned to be part of a land grab. Gabe was not going to let Scientology stop the selling of the city, even though the religion made no effort to "stop" anything they had no knowledge of and were just entering the city as a base for their congregation. Gabe's land grab was about to happen, and he was going to get a huge check.

Gabe had FBI connections to inform them of his competitors and false allegations, but he never informed them of his crimes.

It was clear, Gabe was going to attack Scientology until they were forced to leave Clearwater (this is the source of the "pushing them out of Clearwater" talk) so he could get his check for the plan he had been working on for years.

Around this time, a rogue group of people had infiltrated the Guardian's Office (GO), that was supposed to act as the management entity for Scientology and handle the legal affairs, and these people started attack campaigns at the mayor and started issuing false policies under fake names to attack Gabe and to claim the Church was trying to "take over Clearwater".

This was the plan of those infiltrating the GO to frame the Church in attacking the mayor and thus starting a "war" between both the Church and the City.

After the GO attacked the mayor and his corrupt friends, they took out taxpayer dollars and started hate campaigns against Scientology.

Since the hate campaign was rarely believed, Gabe and his corrupt officials took it to the Courts. They coordinated with failed attorneys.

The failed attorneys coordinated with the anti-Scientology clan at the time, to get them to act as witnesses to impose discriminatory ordinances on Scientology's activities in Clearwater.

As the Church attended every court hearing and listened to every attack spewed at them, they disproved all lies. The attorneys and the city had nothing.

After years of attacks, hearings, and constant corruption by the city against the Church, something happened that would stop any further discrimination from occurring to the Church through the city's corruption.

In 1993, after every ordinance was looked over by the United States Court of Appeals for the Eleventh Circuit, they were found unconstitutional.

"Explicit evidence that the city commission conducted its legislative process from beginning to end with the intention of singling out Scientology for burdensome regulation."
United States Court of Appeals for the Eleventh Circuit

When the Court of Appeals went into the explanation further, the Court stated:

"The record shows a widespread political movement, apparently driven by an upsurge of sectarian fervor that was intent on driving Scientology from Clearwater. It also shows that various members of the commission had made their affiliation with that movement known to the public in the plainest terms possible, not only in the official legislative record leading to adoption of the ordinances but also in documents concerning unrelated government activity and in extemporaneous remarks."
United States Court of Appeals for the Eleventh Circuit

Did the corrupt mayor and his fellow corrupt officials stop there?
No. They attempted to have the U.S. Supreme Court review the case

and they declined it.

Then, on May 17, 1995, the City of Clearwater agreed to a settlement with the Church which was: repealing the 1984 charitable solicitation ordinance and the city paying the Church's legal fees.

Lisa McPherson

I can only imagine how Lisa would feel having her death spewed everywhere for the publicity of the apostates of Scientology.

She passed on due to natural causes as determined by Dr. Joan Woods on February 16, 2000.

Lisa suffered a blood clot due to a recent car accident. She was taken to the New Port Richey Hospital and that's when they knew the devastating passing of Lisa.

A previous study was done by Dr. Woods that was found to be unfounded and then was redone in February 2000, which is the one I am providing you.

Somehow, this has become a way for the anti-Scientology clan to make money and publicity off a lady's death. This is just because she was a Scientologist, and it fits their agenda.

AFFIDAVIT OF AMENDMENT TO MEDICAL CERTIFICATION OF DEATH
FLORIDA

This is the death certificate of Lisa McPherson that explains that she died of natural causes.

"The Pinellas County Florida State Attorney dismissed charges against the Church of Scientology today in a highly publicized case. In November 1998 the State brought charges against the Clearwater based Church, claiming the Church was negligent in caring for one of its parishioners who passed away in December 1995. The decision came after the local Medical Examiner amended the death certificate of Lisa McPherson finding that the death was accidental and not attributable to any actions of the Church or its staff."

"Church of Scientology Exonerated", Issue: June 14, 2000, Pinellas County, FL – PRNewswire

I have included the Lisa McPherson case official decision in the

Documents section of this book. Please refer to it as it has the official statement of 'N O L L E P R O S E Q U I' for the Church of Scientology.

This means that the prosecution has decided to leave it as if charges were never filed against the Church.

Here is the exact statement from the document:

"You will please enter a Nolle Prosequi as to the Church of Scientology Flag Service Organization, Inc., in the above-entitled cause due to the State's inability to prove critical forensic and causation issues beyond and to the exclusion of a reasonable doubt, as a consequence of the Medical Examiner's change of opinion which is reflected in the Amendment of the Death Certificate and Amendment of the Autopsy report dated February 16, 2000."

Bernie McCabe, State Attorney Sixth Judicial Circuit of Florida & Douglas E. Crow Executive Assistant State Attorney, June 12, 2000

There should not be anyone pushing her name through the mud and all for profit.

Get a grip on reality here.

When a court goes through the evidence and comes out with a decision. It is final. It is not up for debate. You should trust our legal system and not play the legal systems for publicity stunts.

As Rinder states it perfectly on June 14, 2000:

"We are very pleased that the State Attorney's office took the appropriate action in dismissing the case once they had the opportunity to review all the evidence. This is a watershed that marks the end of an era of distrust and misunderstanding.

"We thoroughly investigated the matter, looked at the evidence,

called in the leading experts and presented the information to the Medical Examiner. She reviewed the information and changed the death certificate and the State Attorney's Office did the responsible thing. They could have just waited for the court to rule on the pending motions to dismiss the charges - one based on the destruction of exculpatory evidence by the Medical Examiner's Office and the other based on constitutional grounds.

"A lot of false allegations were made over the past few years. But that's history now. That is why we have been working so hard not just on finding out what really happened with Lisa but to also improve relations here so there will never be any misunderstandings like this in the future.

"Lisa McPherson's death was a tragedy that saddened Scientologists more than anyone. The objective science has proven Lisa McPherson's death was an accident and unavoidable. She died of a pulmonary embolism (blood clot in the lungs). Over 100,000 Americans die each year from a pulmonary embolism and in those cases, as here, it is always a shocking experience to those who loved the deceased since pulmonary embolisms are silent killers, virtually unpredictable and not preventable.

"Unfortunately, a few people saw fit to capitalize on the death of a member of our religion in the most unseemly way possible. They invented all manner of stories about Ms. McPherson, covered extensively in the media, which were proven to be untrue."

"We thus endeavored to do two things for both the resolution of these charges and the good of the community,

"First, we presented all objective evidence we had to the State Attorney, allowing him to review it in as neutral an atmosphere as possible. Second, we embarked on a program to bring greater understanding and harmony to our relationships with the community to end the era of distrust -- by both sides -- so any incident in the future could be handled in a way that would prevent a similar injustice and huge waste of time and money. And we have made great strides in this regard."

Rinder is playing you. He knows what happened in the McPherson case. He stated the truth above.

Nobody knew more about the McPherson case than the prosecutor, judge, jury, and the medical examiners (after corruption was exposed and pushed aside).

One of the most widely reported claims was that Ms. McPherson suffered a 50-pound weight loss while in the Church's care. In fact, the evidence now shows she lost no weight. Allegations had also been made that Ms. McPherson was dehydrated, and that this had contributed to her death. Evidence provided by numerous experts showed that Ms. McPherson was not dehydrated, and scientific literature shows dehydration has never in medical history caused a pulmonary embolism.

Again, this is another lie thrown down the chute.

There is no "story" now that the truth is out.

Do not continue this story and let McPherson rest in peace.

Like Rinder states about McPherson's aunt and putting it to rest:

"We expect the distant aunt of Lisa McPherson to drop her civil case,

"She has testified she only wanted to find out what happened to Lisa, and now she knows. Her case has become a forum used by hate mongers to pursue their own agenda in a morbid celebration over the death of a person they never knew, but despised anyway because of her chosen religion. It is time to let Lisa's friends -- those who loved and cared for her -- have closure on this matter rather than having to fight the efforts of those trying to use her death as a means for gold digging."

Mike Rinder, June 14, 2000

I hope Rinder, Remini, and all the other hatemongers pushing McPherson's death stop. The information is out, and it cannot be undone.

Using someone's death as a means of attacking others is insane. Like Rinder states, it is a morbid celebration of a person they have never met. Why the hell would they continue to "celebrate" her death and broadcast it on A&E?

I think it is time to stand up to these bullies and let them know that attacking a religion for someone's death is evil. As well as disseminating her death to make money.

Clearwater was the grounds for all of this.

The Money Scheme

I wanted to give you some details on the money aspect of the Lisa McPherson case for the opposition of Scientology.

This was a way to make some fast cash while attacking Scientology and slamming a lady's death.

The apostates never met or never knew McPherson. She was just a target for their baseless attacks and a way to get back at Scientology for expelling them for their violations and breaking the law.

"Her case has become a forum used by hate mongers to pursue their own agenda in a morbid celebration over the death of a person they never knew, but despised anyway because of her chosen religion. It is time to let Lisa's friends—those who loved and cared for her -- have closure on this matter rather than having to fight the efforts of those trying to use her death as a means for gold digging."

Mike Rinder, June 14, 2000

McPherson did not deserve these attacks. She did not need to be made into a publicity stunt for the ASC. She did not need to be used to make fast cash.

Would you want your family member's death used to make money and fame? Would you allow someone to use someone's death to smear a religion for prejudice and assumptions?

How does someone sleep peacefully knowing that they attacked a lady's death and assumed the cause was her religion due to their own prejudice?

I would like to really understand what makes it acceptable to do this to someone.

But the anti-Scientology clan are found to go after those with lots of money for their gold digging.

The key part of this attack campaign was Ken Dandar, the attorney for the "wrongful death suit" opened by McPherson's distant aunt, was part of a picketing against Scientology in Clearwater on March 9, 1997.

The hateful aunt opened this case "wanting to find out the cause of her death". But this included every single frame you could imagine towards her religion. Her aunt saw this as an opportunity to go after the Church now that her niece's death occurred.

"On March 9, 1997, I met attorney Ken Dandar for the first time

when I participated in a picket in Clearwater, Florida, against the Church of Scientology. Mr. Dandar had an extensive discussion … at that meeting in my presence to learn about the pursuit of other Scientology corporations and church leaders as a litigation tactic to 'go after' Scientology."
Robert Minton, Affidavit

Robert Minton had associated with many anti-Scientology clan members since 1995 and was invited to come join the picket against Scientology in Clearwater. He accepted the invite.

When he was picketing in 1997 with Dandar, they came up with a plan around that time to go after Scientology.

Minton was so committed to the anti-Scientology clan members that he supported them first by opening an office in Downtown Clearwater next to the dining hall of the Scientology staff. This is where he would have daily pickets with bullhorns yelling obscenities at parishioners and staff of the Church and harassing them every chance they had.

Minton was the "ATM" for the anti-Scientology clan. He was able to loan money to go after Scientology and do it without question. If there was an expense that an apostate could not cover but it was completely against Scientology, a check would be written out immediately.

"Until October 1997 my financial involvement against Scientology was limited to the Wollersheim litigation. At that time, I decided that the Lisa McPherson wrongful death case would be a far more effective centerpiece for me and I contacted Mr. Dandar in October 1997 and offered to loan the Estate $100,000 to defray costs and expenses so this case could become a vehicle to attack Scientology on a broad scale."
Robert Minton, Affidavit

There was something that made Scientology seem so bad to Minton. There was nothing Scientology could do to explain themselves to him; he was already deprogrammed by the apostates. They leached onto him.

Minton started loaning the death case money and to be paid back in full when Scientology was charged, and the winnings were collected.

"That $100,000 and all subsequent amounts, up to a total of $2,050,000, I loaned to the Estate was specifically meant for covering the expenses of litigating the wrongful death case. It was not a personal loan to Mr. Dandar and was not to be spent for other purposes or other cases. The agreement I had with the Estate was that if the case was won or favorably settled, I would get my money back (with no interest) once the Estate's expenses were covered."

Robert Minton, Affidavit

Therefore, Minton and Dandar were working together with the rest of the clan trying to spin the truth and frame the Church for the death of McPherson. They wanted the big paycheck, and they wanted the case to close with the Church losing.

They tried to cover their tracks. Dandar making statements and then contradicting them.

"Following receipt of my $100,000, Mr. Dandar sent me a letter telling me I would have no participation in the control of the litigation. This self-serving statement quickly became untrue, as Mr. Dandar immediately began consulting me about the conduct of the litigation, briefing me on confidential information from the case, sending me copies of deposition and hearing transcripts, and calling me for advice. His statements concerning case control became increasingly untrue throughout my involvement in the

case when Mr. Dandar would do things in the litigation designed to satisfy my wishes and thus get more money from me."
Robert Minton, Affidavit

Dandar thus made a false statement to act as "evidence" if Scientology caught onto Dandar and Minton's schemes. They coordinated on every step of the case. It was horrendous.

This was a case of money for the clan. Minton geared everything towards this purpose. He paid the clan members to move to Clearwater, he paid them for their false testimonies, and their other activities in relation to attacking the Church.

He was destined to go after the Church. This was not something you could deny. This was real to him and the clan.

"In October 1999, Mr. Dandar incorporated the organization under the name Lisa McPherson Trust (LMT). I was the President and sole shareholder. Mr. Dandar organized the LMT as a for-profit entity but he told me that we would reincorporate it as a non-profit when it was time to distribute funds from the wrongful death case."
Robert Minton, Affidavit

Therefore, the LMT was there for profit. This backs the statement that it was there to make money off McPherson's death, if the Church was charged with a murder.

But Scientology was on their tail as their legal counsel spotted various red flags about Dandar and Minton and the Estate's financial status.

Dandar was rarely focused on the evidence, rarely focused on the actual case, and was not ever focused on McPherson. He was focused on forcing the court to charge the Church unjustly and against the evidence supplied.

This, to Dandar and Minton, was a big publicity stunt with massive amounts of money at stake. This is evil. But they continued with this tactic.

"Mr. Dandar was very happy about my setting up the LMT, as it was going to get "Scientology onto the front page of the newspaper" and help create a favorable jury pool for the case."
Robert Minton, Affidavit

If this were to be pulled through, the Church would have been framed for McPherson's death with the facts not adding up. It was essentially going to force the court to incorrectly charge the Church as a publicity stunt.

But this was just the jury pool of the case. They still needed the witnesses to testify against Scientology using doctored testimonies and their hate for the Church. They looked no further than the clan members that were available for the task due to their unemployment and their dedication to make money from attacking their former religion.

Minton coordinated the payment of the witnesses and the collecting of them in rapid fashion.

"I gathered the most vocal Scientology critics and most of the anti-Scientology witnesses under the umbrella of the LMT. I paid the witnesses through my funding of the LMT and put other critics on the LMT Board of Advisors. Because I was funding both the case and its witnesses, the wrongful death case and the LMT became virtually interchangeable."
Robert Minton, Affidavit

So, it was rigged either way for Minton and the witnesses to make money. They were being paid for perjury and for their hate against

Scientology. They had nothing to do with McPherson and everything to do with their hate for the Church.

The money he was dishing out to the clan members were adding up to 'incredible' amounts.

"I paid for Mr. Prince to move to Clearwater and loaned him $50,000 to buy a home. I arranged for Mr. Prince to work for Mr. Dandar as his expert. He was paid $5,000 per month with the money I gave Mr. Dandar. I had Stacy Brooks set up the LMT and paid her $5,000 a month as the LMT president. Both were being paid by me, one through Mr. Dandar and the other through the LMT. In the spring of 2000, I had Mr. Prince transfer from Dandar & Dandar to the LMT, but his salary of $5,000 remained the same. David Cecere came to Clearwater to be executive director of the LMT at $5,000 per month and later, after his employment at the LMT was terminated, he became a Scientology "expert" for Mr. Dandar in the wrongful death case. Ms Brooks gave disaffected former Scientologist Teresa Summers a job at the LMT earning $3,500 per month, after Mr. Dandar had put her on the witness list in the wrongful death case. I put Gerry Armstrong on the Advisory Board of the LMT after Mr. Dandar put him on his witness list. I had earlier given Mr. Armstrong $100,000. I later learned he used these funds to forward an attack on Scientology and pursue a lawsuit against David Miscavige and various Scientology entities. Others on the "Advisory Board" of LMT included Ken Dandar, Dan Leipold, Dell Liebreich, Keith Hensen, Grady Ward, and Arnie Lerma, all of whom I financially supported in their litigation with Scientology."

Robert Minton, Affidavit

Yes, it is a bit to state by Minton but, it explains every single inch of the financial support he gave to the witnesses and who he had on his "Board of Advisers" of the LMT and the wrongful death case against Scientology.

Minton and Dandar and the rest of the squad were after Scientology to get money and fame. This was never about McPherson; it was about going after Scientology.

McPherson did not deserve to be slandered throughout the many years she has been gone. Her family does not deserve the constant attacks. Her religion is not responsible for her death but, they still care about getting the truth out there. The truth was already discovered in 2000 with the death record but the clan chose to ignore it.

But, to the apostates there is never anything right that the Church can do after it expelled them for their crimes and did not look back.

Let us all put this attack campaign against McPherson to rest.

Do not participate in any more publicity stunts, scare tactics, and other stunts played out by the clan and their tabloid connections. It is all corruption, and we need to ensure that the clan are frowned upon, especially when someone's death is permitted to be smeared for close to 20 years.

You may be able to find some altered pictures, documents, and other "proof" that the clan developed to save face. These documents were not ever in the courts and were never going to be.

It is time to let McPherson rest and stop dragging the death of a person whose religion you did not like, through the mud for no sane reason.

DISCONNECTION

**"I left. I walked out of the Church. I walked away from my family,
knowing I was walking away from my family."**
Mike Rinder

By now I am sure you have heard something along the lines of separating family members and friends. I wanted to provide you with more information on the subject so that you did not make your decision based on noise.

Those who have been expelled from the Church of Scientology are not happy with that decision, understandably. I understand that they are not happy with this decision because their intention was to cause as much harm as possible and as much chaos as possible to the Church, its members, their friends, and family all because they are Scientologists. The unstable do not like when their power is taken from them.

L. Ron Hubbard developed a technology that makes the person more in control of their life without having to be connected to toxic people. This technology is publicly available and is used by those in the Church and outside of the Church. Mr. Hubbard released this technology to ensure that people had a way out of toxic relationships using their fundamental rights as human beings to give and receive communication at will. He also mentions that if one has the right to communicate then also one has the right to not communicate nor receive communication from another. Scientologists are no different and should be afforded with the same rights as everybody else.

"Perhaps the most fundamental right of any being is the right to communicate. Without this freedom, other rights deteriorate. Communication, however, is a two-way flow. If one has the right to communication, the one must also have the right to not receive communication from another. ... The term 'disconnection' is defined as a self-determined decision made by an individual that he is not going to be connected to another. ... With our tech of handle or disconnect, we are, in actual fact, doing nothing different that any society or group or marriage down through thousands of years. ... We cannot afford to deny Scientologists that basic freedom that is granted to everyone else: the right to choose whom one wishes to communicate with or not communicate with."

L. Ron Hubbard, Introduction to Scientology Ethics

The only people that are raging against this technology are the ones that will not get their life together and realize that they are the problem, not the other person. For one to separate from another, or disconnect from another, one needs to attempt to consistently handle the person on the other end that they are having trouble with. When there is no change from the person that they are having trouble with and the actions continue and possibly even escalate into an even worse situation, one makes the decision on one's own that he or she will not be connected to that person until that person changes by stopping their attacks, harassment, and general toxicity. Scientologists value their time, they believe that every moment should be spent hanging out with family, improving their lives, and most of all helping others.

What is the viewpoint in relation to those who are spreading the noise surrounding this technology to make it sound bad? You are taking the power from them to make your life worse and to cause chaos in your life. You are improving and they are not, in fact they do not see this as improvement, they see this as a threat to their survival. For some reason, they believe that as you get happier and more successful, they will be exposed for having prevented you from doing these things. The unstable tend to take people successes as threats, if you need an example of this just look at what Leah Remini is doing to others who are genuinely helping others and who are successful.

This is a topic of conversation when it comes to Mike Rinder because he used this technology the wrong way and he knows it. He used it on his family because they are Scientologists and he no longer wanted to be a Scientologist due to the wrongdoings he did to the Church, these wrongdoings were about to be exposed in an investigation that was ongoing when he failed to show back up at his place of residence where his wife was waiting his arrival back into the country after being in the United Kingdom.

As a note, when the Church officials do an investigation into a matter concerning members and their actions in the Church, one can still help the religion in a limited capacity. While this investigation was undergoing, he was allowed to leave the country on a mission in the UK where he was assisting the Church's Spokesperson with tasks surrounding answering reporters questions the right way and offering tours to them to any of the Church's facilities and the locations of their supported humanitarian campaigns.

Rinder fails to mention this to you and his small number of supporters. He claims the Church did wrong to him which caused him to go crazy, this is not true and is an attempt at placing the blame on a religion that only gave him numerous opportunities to change. He did not take these opportunities and he disconnected from his family. That should be the end of the story, but if you know anything about him, that is just the start of a campaign of lies to bury the truth.

The only communication he had after he arrived in the US was to a Church official to do a property swap. Meaning, he had Church property as in a phone, and other materials, that he wanted to return in exchange for his minimal personal belongings and to have them shipped to him. He also mentioned to this official that he would like to offer his wife to come with him, which she declined because she would be leaving her family behind and her religion. Obviously, he left his family, and he left his religion. He must have known due to the religion's incredible technology in investigations, in truth and in ethics that his wrongdoings would be found out and he was not willing to take any responsibility for them. The responsibility would have been to confront the court of law and he knows it.

After he left his family with no further communication, his daughter, his son, his now ex-wife and his brother (who lives in Australia) flew out to see him to find out what occurred and to see if they could mend this situation so that they could still be in touch – even though he did not want to be a Scientologist. He raged at the idea and assaulted his ex-wife in front of the family members that came to see him.

His assault caused his ex-wife, the mother of his two children, Ben, and Taryn, to have to live with permanent harm done. You must ask yourself, why would he do such a thing?

Of course, after that unhinged incident, he knew he was in serious trouble, and he was already in the pockets of those who oppose the Church. He decided to call *Tampa Bay Times* and make up a story of how his family members came to attack him and he had to defend himself. No responsibility Rinder, that is what I like to call him. He had to make this story before the Church and his family had a chance to say anything about the matter, even though they would not make a comment because it was a personal matter and would be addressed between them (that was until he published the attack in the newspaper). He believed that if he did not make this story quick, his followers might see the truth about him. If they saw the truth about him, he would lose his livelihood in attacking the church he once was part of and that his family is still a part of.

The narrative that one would disconnect based on religious belief and practice is rubbish. While it does not happen in the Church, it does not mean it is not happening outside of it. Rinder is a prime example of this in action, he did disconnect from his family based on their religious beliefs and practices. You cannot argue with that.

As if we needed another example, his son was fighting cancer and he wanted nothing to do with his son and did not care at all about his fight. Rinder's statements to the contrary in public were completely different and the Church called him out for that as he kept dragging the Church into why he did not care about his son and how people were preventing him from communicating (even though that is all his family was trying to get from him, a communication). He tried to keep this campaign going and it continued to get shot down with the truth.

When desperation was so high (as the truth was being exposed), Rinder spoke to his best friend, Mark Rathbun, who gave him an idea to stage a camera shot in front of one of the Church's religious retreats in Clearwater, Florida, knowing that Rinder is trespassed from all properties belonging to the Church. The Church's security would inform him that he was not allowed on any of the premises, since he would not leave, the Church involved the Clearwater Police Department, and Rinder staged his shot to try to get a police officer to go into the religious retreat to "find his son", as was the purpose of the stunt. The officer had to go along, and the Church welcomed the officer with open arms and when the officer went to meet Ben Rinder, Rinder's son, to ask him if he wanted to see his father, Ben said the following:

"...in 2009, I think, I was in the sauna and two policemen come into the sauna—but, you know— "We need to see you." So, I, "Okay." So, I got up out—went out of the sauna. Basically said, "Your dad is at the front of the building, and he wants to see you. He's waiting for you." And, you know, for a moment you can

think, "Oh he—maybe there's a bit of compassion there or care." But then you think, "Well, wait a sec. What's the only reason he would be standing in front of the Fort Harrison with a camera crew trying to come and get me, getting the police involved?" He's just trying to make himself right maybe or prove a point like, "Look how bad they treated us" and to create a fabricated story or something. And I said, "I want nothing to do with him. I don't want to talk to him. I don't want to see him. I want nothing to do with him. I'm living my life and I'm figuring it out and he can live his life and he's on his own with that. I want nothing to do with it." And they said, "Okay, so you want nothing to do with him?" "I want nothing to do with him." Like, "Okay." They left.

"He doesn't care about me, he doesn't. If I had died five years ago, it would have just been like, "Shoot, I need another angle now" to, you know, cause trouble or whatever. So…I'm perfectly happy with him not knowing anything about me. I don't, I don't care. I don't live my life trying to, you know, prove him, prove something. Doesn't matter to me.

"Other than showing up at the front of the Fort Harrison, he has never contacted me. I don't think he's ever called me in my life. Like, and I'm not talking about just since he left. I'm saying I don't think he's ever called me.

"He's totally separated himself from us [our family] and we are all in touch. We are all doing what we've been doing, moving on with life.

"We were all in the same space—like here's all of us in this circle. We are all still here, except for him—he's the only one that moved out of this hypothetical space. I think that defines

disconnection. We're all doing exactly what we were doing, what we've always been doing. We're doing better and we're totally fine and I think he's the odd one out."

The only reason he speaks about his family is because they are Scientologists and that they know the truth about his actions. They have the right, and he knows that, to state the truth, even now that they have been attacked viciously. That is why he is so determined to pile on as many narratives surrounding them so that the unstable who follow him never get to hear the truth because they do not believe it.

This viciousness is his life. What you see around him and what you see he talks about is his doing but flipped against the Church. You will never hear him say one thing good about the Church, his investors would lose it on him. These investors are old people with retirement funds, investment funds, and those individuals that have been in bad places that have been affected by the positive change the Church has helped make for society. What do I mean by that? I know the drug lords do not like the Church because the Church is supports one of the largest nongovernmental drug education programs which causes those who invest in drugs and who push drugs to be exposed, their profits to dry up with no new customers, and eventually their whole operation shuts down. I know human traffickers hate Scientology because Scientologists are informing people of their thirty inalienable human rights throughout the world and bringing awareness to this important topic. Now, am I saying that these individuals are funding Rinder and Remini? I believe I am saying that Rinder and Remini have some "hidden" connections with some bad people that hate the Church's vision for a better world.

So, his family and friends are waiting for him to get straight in his life before it is too late, as he is getting old and that is the harsh reality of life. If he does not change, that will be on his conscience and not on theirs. His family and friends have tried everything in their power to wake him up, nothing has helped change his behavior and his decision to not be part of their lives due to being Scientologists.

As I do not want to be the only source you get information about disconnection from, I would refer to *Introduction to Scientology Ethics* by L. Ron Hubbard. This is a publicly available book, it has been available since the 60s, and it is a good reference the next time somebody says something about ethics, justice, and related subjects about Scientology.

STARTING A CHURCH

Rinder has some awful ways of communicating that Scientology works, he does not have to start a campaign against the Church to communicate that it works.

What you probably do not know, I believe it is safe to say that you do not know this at all, is that Rinder tried to start his own "independent" Church of Scientology. Just like he is used to doing things rogue, this is a prime example of exactly that mentality. He planned on starting his own church and using fake scripture that he deemed "Scientology".

He did in fact register this entity and miraculously convinced a federal or city official to recognize him as an "independent" Scientology minister. He ended up using this license to marry best friend and anti-Scientologist, Mark Rathbun, and his now wife. In Rinder's church the "parishioners" were all made up of the anti-Scientology crowd, including those that were expelled and we're on the payroll of attacking the Church of Scientology.

If you thought this was the first time a person like Rinder has tried to start something like this, you have not heard of the Anti-Scientology Cult (ASC). I see it fitting that we go over this cult before we dive into what Rinder recently tried.

The ASC is run by a small group of unstable people who have been expelled from the Church of Scientology for their wrongdoings and their crimes against the laws of the land. The Church believes *nobody* is above the law and therefore tells the person, while expelling them, to turn themselves in and get right with the law. The person expelled rarely does this; I should really say they never do this. Those same people are now attacking the Church for expelling them which has left them powerless in their path to try to take over the Church and steal parishioner donations, not to mention also try to alter the scripture.

Rathbun went over this small group of people when he spoke out against Leah Remini for her blackmail tactics and attempt to get him on her payroll and thus become her slave. He decided against joining Remini and Rinder and instead exposed the whole operation on YouTube for the world to see. Does that mean Rathbun is a Scientologist now? No, in his videos he never states that he is a Scientologist, nor does he state that he is trying to rejoin the Church. This is a narrative spread around Rathbun's campaign to expose what happens in the ASC and Rinder and Remini claim he is a Scientologist to somehow "discredit" the truth, as Remini and Rinder have constantly tried to demonize the Church. The Church has also shared his videos to disseminate the message for the world to see that they have been telling the truth the entire time about this operation against them. This would tie into the false narrative that the Church is working with Rathbun, but he is just exposing the operation that is attacking Scientology.

"ATTENTION OUTERBANKERS: We have long since had RULES AND GUIDELINES. Go to the upper right-hand corner where there is a link called Description. In the rules, we do not permit trashing or demeaning or disparaging posts of our hero activist leaders, Mike Rinder and Tony Ortega. If you attack the main activists your posts will be deleted, you will be warned. If you do not agree to this, then you do not belong on Outerbanks."

I remember explaining the ASC in a few my books, but I have also found new information about current operations in this small declining group that is now run mainly by Remini and Rinder. It is funded by a former sex worker who also goes by over ten different names and is currently referred to as Karen. Karen has a husband that goes by Jeff. Karen and Jeff, mainly Karen, scrounge up money from various people that they can easily infect with lies about Scientology and empty promises based on these lies. Karen sets her targets on those with a retirement fund or an investment account. This money is then taken into the ASC and then dispersed *immediately* to those that followed the rules in the group and were respectful to the royalty of the group, commonly referred to in other groups as leaders or executives, but in the ASC, they should be referred to as masters. If you did exactly what you were told and did not speak out against the ASC or its masters, you will be rewarded with money (but not as much as the masters get). What do they deliver to the person in return for the money? They butter them up with false progress because they have nothing on the Church, and they know there is no evidence against it. There have been *many* investigations that the ASC has sparked against the religion, and the results of these have found no such evidence (not even an inch) to corroborate what the ASC reports. The ASC will say and do anything for money, that includes file false reports with law enforcement and publicize it as if it were "successful" or it is "ongoing".

But you may not know that this group was tried before and was completely wiped out from the inside. It is happening to the current version as well; people are speaking out from the inside of what they refer to as "Leah's cult". The first version was around in the 80s and the person responsible for that version was a man expelled around that time for inventing his own scriptures and would pass them off as L. Ron Hubbard to cause harm to Scientologists, he believed he knew more than Mr. Hubbard. He was trusted to ensure the correct delivery of Scientology scriptures in counseling sessions, he would give direction to the counselors, also known as auditors, that would intentionally cause longer sessions and could have caused lots of mental problems as well as spiritual problems for thousands of Scientologists. In one instance he intentionally caused his ex lots of trouble in counseling sessions using what he wrote as an "expert". His name was David and this group fell hard and fast. The Church caused its downfall by expanding and continuing to help as many people as possible with *real* Scientology and not the fake ASC scriptures claiming to be "Scientology". This is where the "confidential material" rumor online stemmed from – these fake scriptures passed off as "L. Ron Hubbard" and the "creation theory".

"And what about David's knowledge of the "secret- unreleased" upper upper OT levels? Well, I remember the time in 1984 when Mayo released his version of "OT 8", and what a FLOP. It was given to only a couple of PCs [preclears, person being counseled] and you never saw two more distressed PCs in your life. And that was the last we heard of David bringing out new "upper levels!" That's a little story you maybe never heard about."

Jon Zegel, Former ASC Spokesperson

This now dissolved group of people caused a lot of harm for people as they were using made-up scripture. Mr. Hubbard wrote about the importance of using *real* Scientology and not the alterations as mentioned in the statement below.

"My earnest advice is: Only deal with or associate with those organizations licensed by RTC [Religious Technology Center] and auditors in good standing with the Church; close your ears to false statements made by bad hats and thus really clear the planet."

L. Ron Hubbard, Ron's Journal 38, "Today and Tomorrow: The Proof", New Year's Eve 1983

With this statement by Mr. Hubbard, you should consider the former ASC spokesperson also stated their intentions and the reality of where they are at now. It is gruesome and for the people involved who thought the ASC was telling the truth – they need to come find out about the *real* application of Scientology technology.

> **"Needless to say we have all been through an ordeal together - leaving the Church, the quote heyday unquote of the field, and then the reality of what we actually ended up with in the field.**
>
> **"And that's not much to speak of. A heap of ashes might be an apt description.**
>
> **"I don't think this fact comes to you as any great surprise. All you have to do is look around and you can see for yourself that this is true.**
>
> **"But the purpose of this tape is not to tell you what you already know. ...**
>
> **"1. The public that we were going to go after were Scientologists primarily on lines at the church...We were mainly interested in those who already knew Scientology worked and were ripe for the plucking.**
>
> **"2. We knew that unless we promised standard tech [the intended application of Scientology scriptures] we couldn't get many people to really leave the church. Mind you, I'm not saying Standard Tech was ever delivered - I'm saying we HAD to promise it. We knew that we could only pull in the Church public if we promised good standard tech.**
>
> **3. This is where David ... came in. We pushed the line that**

[David] was the highest trained terminal in the field and that he had data on the upper levels that no one in the church had, thereby giving the field its own attraction. A classic "hidden data line" - it tuned in perfectly with the "inside" or "hidden stories" about the ship [Scientology's ship that delivers advanced services] and Int [international management of the Church of Scientology] and so on.

But the more data that I got in this research, the more I find [David]'s assertions to be false. But at the time I ate it up hook, line and sinker and sold it like gospel truth. And it was very convincing.

And what about David's knowledge of the "secret- unreleased" upper OT levels? Well, I remember the time in 1984 when Mayo released his version of "OT 8", and what a FLOP. It was given to only a couple of PCs [definition in back of book] and you never saw two more distressed PCs in your life. And that was the last we heard of David bringing out new "upper levels!" That's a little story you maybe never heard about.

4. Another part of the strategy was to give you the impression that people were leaving the church in droves. It's funny how people don't like to take the plunge all by themselves, but if you can assure them that others just like them have taken the leap they feel more reassured. My tapes were to reassure you that it was OK to leave the church."

Jon Zegel, Former ASC Spokesperson

Based on these points shared by the spokesperson for this dissolved group, you see the plan for this "new" version. The plan has not changed,

Remini and Rinder are banking on the fact that people in day and age have no idea what happened in the 80s and will try this again. They have been trying to do this since Remini was expelled and they have not been able to make a dent in it and they are hitting a brick wall. The ASC knows it is hitting a brick wall and has no way around it. Just like Jon Zegel, Former ASC Spokesperson, went through. That brick wall is reality setting in. Nobody took the "plunge", and it was just those who had already been expelled and dismissed that joined the ASC – that was the reality they never shared with you.

The Church has been expanding like none other and has been utilizing the technological advancements of this time to ensure Scientology is being delivered at the level that is the most optimum and at the speed at which it was intended. Why do I say this? The individuals I have mentioned in this chapter have tried to halt the expansion of the Church and have tried to destroy every inch of the scripture in Scientology so that it no longer works. These people *almost* succeeded, almost is the key word there. They failed thankfully because of David Miscavige. Mr. Miscavige was onto their plan while they were in the Church and caught them in the act of altering the scriptures. Specifically, four people who were once part of the first version of the ASC and who were one of the sources of income for the attackers. They once had access to the scripture while in the Church, and they went to town.

The ASC up to this point in 2007, the point of when the Church announced that all the scriptures were looked over and verified after referencing it with every page and recording of Mr. Hubbard's through handwritten words and reel to reel tapes which culminated a 25 year project headed by Mr. Miscavige himself, believed that if they could just continue a false information campaign that the Church did not work that there might be some people that would believe that. But that did not work, and the Church continued to blast off in expansion and a record amount of people started actively participating in Scientology and this occurred due to this release, from all around the world. This was *huge* and started causing another problem with the buildings needing to be equipped to handle the added growth. With this release of all the writings and recorded lectures of Mr. Hubbard's verified, ready for worldwide consumption with a wholly digital publishing powerhouse and translating it all in many languages – the attackers lost, and they could not do anything about it. They were expelled. They felt powerless, including Rinder.

Then came the announcement of the completion of the next phase of Scientology technology. This included the verification of all steps to spiritual awareness and advanced the delivery of spiritual counseling – auditing – with a new e-meter (a tool used to guide the auditor to the source of trouble in a person's life – full definition in the back of the book). This involved a team of over 1,000 trainees going to Clearwater, Florida, to get through the entire program where they would learn how to correctly deliver Scientology through their courses, counseling, supervision of services, and other vital functions. It started in early 2013 and ended in November 2013 and was celebrated with the opening of the Scientology Cathedral.

Rinder was not around for the technological release in November of 2013 and funny enough, Remini was expelled in early 2013. Expansion had become too much for Remini and she had to leave, she failed to take responsibility for her actions because she knew she was trying to impede the religion (being a plant by the end of her stint in the Church for Rinder). The same goes with every attacker to date.

This technological release changed the religion entirely, it changed it in the sense that Mr. Hubbard intended for Scientology to be delivered a certain way, a very effective way and utilizing all technological advances of the day and age. People who were once in the religion are coming back like never before and if you walk into a Church, they will tell you stories of people traveling for *many* hours and even days to get to their local Church and find out how they can get some help. These actions alone anger the people attacking the Church because they know they have failed in impeding people from getting the help that they need.

He can continue to dream up plans to try to take over the Church (including the failed lawsuit of $1 billion dollars that he tried to dream up and present) and they will continue to fail. The more he mentions Scientology, the more sane people walk into the doors of the locations worldwide to find out more. Maybe he is doing this to help the Church secretly, because honestly that is what it is doing.

Back to the attempt at starting an "independent church" in 2009 to 2010, he knew at that moment in time that Scientology works and that he knew deep down inside that he committed the grossest violations to the law and against the Church's scriptures. But instead of taking responsibility for his actions in the Church, he decided to make his own church and he failed at that. And once he had failed at making this church, he decided to go full time on attacking Scientology – his family's religion.

So, the Church will continue to open new locations to help even more people, it will continue to educate people on their human rights, it will continue to support drug rehabilitation and educate people on the dangers of drugs, and so many other aspects. Rinder will continue to ignore his family, friends and the world declining around him.

The faster one snaps back into reality the faster one can get moving on things that need to be addressed in this crazy world. Getting wrapped up in false narratives and witch hunts against people due to false reports is a waste of time that could be devoted to helping people with problems in their everyday lives and those affected by natural disasters.

TAX EXEMPTION

"And it is also David Miscavige who made the tax exemption by the IRS possible. It is he who personally walked into the front lobby of the IRS National Headquarters and through two years of persistent work, ultimately brought about a peace with the IRS that had seemed impossible. But perhaps the most telling point is this: it was the IRS targeting individual Scientologists, merely because they were Scientologists, that motivated him the most in this endeavor. Again, he didn't take credit for this, he has told me many times that he felt it was his duty to all Scientologists to carry this off so they would be free to practice their religion just like those of other faiths."

Mike Rinder, Affidavit

By now you understand that Scientology is a new subject and has not had 100 years under its belt to get the word out about it and answer people's questions. Therefore, we must go over tax exemption status of the Church, this is an area that is not touched on as it would be commonly understood without the confusions and noise that has been spread around it.

Mike Rinder takes his fantasy of "authority" in the Church and makes it seem like he knows everything there is to know about tax exemption in the religion and the "secrets" (he just came up with) about the attainment of it.

In the 80s Scientology and its members were being attacked due to their assumed (based on false information) religious beliefs and practices and they were being audited, bank accounts being frozen and various other tactics to keep the Church from obtaining this status. Why? Some in the Internal Revenue Service (IRS) were being fed false information about the

Church by those who aim to make millions attacking it. Obtaining this status would legitimize Scientology rightfully as a religion, which was already declared a bona fide religion by the United States Supreme Court *before* the IRS investigation, and afford it the same privileges as other religions – new and old.

The Church originally ignored their attempts by brushing them off to attack and started sending documentation as is necessary for the standard IRS exemption process and they would not be reviewed but instead sent back immediately. The IRS representatives responsible for this process were not interested in abiding by the standard process. These representatives had their sights on making sure Scientology never had tax-exemption, the privilege afforded to other religions, and it was all based on false information given by people trying to make money from their former religion.

With these attacks continuing against the Church by the IRS, Mr. David Miscavige, ecclesiastical leader of the religion, looked at the reality of the situation and noticed that it was not going to stop. The Church started using the legal system to try to figure out what information the IRS was operating from regarding Scientology and its members, as this was preventing the Church from going through the standard tax-exemption procedure. The IRS representatives in charge of these attacks on the Church framed the Church's attempt at getting information as somehow "intimidating" and these representatives made claims in the court of law which were unfounded to try to corroborate these false stories of "intimidation".

It was not until the Church presented all evidence of blatant discrimination and no ill will on their part that the judge started cracking down on the representatives of the IRS and thus the truth started coming out and the representatives that had lied started admitting it.

But, of course, the representatives still believed the lies that were spread about the Church, so they were continuing their inactions on the tax exemption procedure and continue to target Scientologists for their religious beliefs and practices.

No matter what the Church officials shared with the IRS, the matter was still not being taken seriously and was still not moving. Mr. Miscavige monitored the entire situation and did not escalate the situation and only presented solutions to both the IRS representatives and the church officials. No matter what the Church did to attempt to provide information as per the procedure, the IRS did nothing about it.

After a few years of these attacks, Mr. Miscavige took it upon himself to walk into the IRS headquarters and speak to the IRS commissioner personally to handle all situations and two ensure that the IRS new that the Church is taking this *very* seriously and will provide any information requested without *any* consideration or questions asked. From this meeting, the Church provided more than 1,000,000 pages of information with no questions asked and no considerations. These pages explained their beliefs, practices, organizational structure, financial structure, in every facet that needed to be explained for this tax-exempt status.

The IRS eventually concluded in 1993 that the Church of Scientology and its supported humanitarian campaigns are wholly nonprofit organizations and that they qualify for tax-exemption. This investigation took many years and culminated over 1,000,000 pages, which is the largest investigation done by the IRS on any religion to date.

What the apostates will tell you is the complete opposite because they hated that the Church got through to the IRS to go through the standard process regardless of what the IRS thought of the Church. The truth was right in their faces, and they could not deny the Church the privilege they gave to every other religion.

To this date, the Church takes this *very* seriously. The Church meets once a year with IRS officials to go over all the documentation for that year to make sure that it is what they want and to get briefed on any new codes and any special requests.

When the attacks stopped from the IRS with the granting of a tax-exempt status for Scientology, Mr. Miscavige had a milestone event for all Scientologists and their friends and family to attend to get all the information that led up to the attainment of this status. He laid it all out and did not leave any detail out of the briefing. The briefing hit home to every Scientologist in the audience as they could rest easy knowing that they were not going to be attacked by the IRS and that they could practice their religion just like everybody else with the same privileges as those in other faiths.

The briefing was called the war is over and *M*ark Rathbun spoke highly just recently about what Mr. Miscavige spoke about at that event. It was a milestone in Scientology that caused even more people to practice the religion. It also opened the door to even more expansion for the *Church,* as members could get the same benefits as members of other religions do when they donate to future churches*, * church projects *and receiving religious services.*

The donation structure in Scientology is new as it was designed to take into account the various resources that go into delivering Scientology services, including paying the staff, paying the bills, paying rent for the building (if they do not own their own building yet), the forward expansion of the religion, the replenishment of materials used, and various other aspects that go into operating a worldwide religion. This whole structure was looked over by the IRS and approved. If it did not add up, the IRS would have disapproved it.

One of the final misconceptions on this point would be that the IRS gave Scientology tax-exemption before the United States Supreme Court did a separate investigation and found that it was a bona fide religion. The IRS gave tax-exempt status to the Church after they did a separate investigation of the Church and after the Supreme Court came out with their own decision. This is what caused the Church to want the privilege afforded to all religions, because they had just concluded a major investigation by the Supreme Court on whether they are a bona fide religion. Rathbun can also back this up and has backed us up by calling out what Rinder states about it as false.

Rinder wants attention so he will make claims as if he knows the information, but he really does not.

INFANT DAUGHTER

"I know his compassion from personal experience. While Vicki Aznaran makes cruel claims concerning the death of my infant daughter, she does not know what in fact occurred, or if she does, she is simply lying to try to create a false impression. In this time of great personal upset, David and his wife Shelly supported my wife and me beyond what could possibly be expected by anyone – seeing to our personal needs, arranging for the most highly trained auditors to give us spiritual counselling (counseling), arranging plane fares and reservations, helping with the funeral arrangements and making it as easy as possible in every fashion imaginable for us to come through this upsetting time. I resent any implication that has been made to the contrary by Vicki Aznaran – her statements are beneath contempt."

Mike Rinder, Affidavit

I do not wish this on anyone. This experience must have been hard on not only Rinder but his wife at the time.

Mr. David Miscavige, and his wife, Shelly, took this situation very seriously and ensured that Rinder and his wife were taken care of, provided with the best Scientology auditors, arranging plane fares, even including the funeral service. Scientology helped regardless of what Rinder failed to do at the time in the Church because that is what Scientologists do – help. Scientologists do *not* turn away from those who need help and that are going through troubles.

Vicki Aznaran, one of the four people caught by Mr. Miscavige altering the scriptures of L. Ron Hubbard and who later wrote an affidavit exposing the Anti-Scientology Cult's litigation tactics, used her moment of attacking her former religion for money in court to make false statements about not only the Church, but Rinder himself. After all, he was at minimum in the Church and was holding a position that threatened her litigation tactic (he was the legal director).

The Church was *not* required in the slightest to cover the airfare and the travel expenses of Rinder and his wife and anything else they needed to get through during this upsetting time. The Church does not believe one is bad because they are having troubles and need assistance through proper training and correction in the area in which they are responsible. The Church also cares for every Sea Organization member and every Scientologist.

As I do not like to talk about people personal tragedies, regardless of if they are attacking me because I have decency, I will state that, from my view with the information provided to me, the Church went above and beyond what would have been asked in this situation. Specifically, Mr. Miscavige and his wife.

May this child rest in peace.

CHRISTIE RINDER

Mike Rinder's now wife, Christie Collbran-Rinder, has a side to her that was unleashed when she paired with him.

Psychotic behavior tends to latch onto another who was once known for being friendly, caring and overall social and turn the person towards psychotic behavior because it is "what feels right".

One of the things Christie did when she first left the Church of Scientology was call her mother and scream at her to force her to leave the religion. She wanted her mother to leave with her and abandon the family just as she did. Of course, the mother declined, and Christie has not been heard from since.

Christie has since been part of groups with people wanted by the FBI for cyberterrorism, worked alongside inciters of murder, and so many others.

Her mother says the following about her:

"Our family was going along this path. Christie was with us and then all of a sudden, she took a big U-turn. And it was her decision.

"When Christie first called me and we had our first talk about what she was doing, it started out sort of, you know, okay. And then it ratcheted up and ratcheted up and—to the point where Christie was screaming in my ear. And, and I was like—really, I was traumatized, I really was traumatized. I wasn't expecting it. And it went on and on and on—her screaming at me about

various things that she wanted to get across to me that she thought was bad. And then—and then telling me how stupid I was.

"She thought that she could talk to me and tell me the things that she was going to tell me that would make me think Scientology—I should abandon it. And that was what she wanted to accomplish—that's what she was trying to do. It didn't work. It actually backfired on her. It's like, "No Christie, I'm sorry, this—this isn't going to happen. I'm not going to leave Scientology because you—for whatever reasons you're telling me that I should—after being in Scientology for decades, and having it change my life for the better throughout the entire time, I'm not going to abandon it because of what you say. Especially in the tone of voice you're saying it and sort of the—just shrill screaming. You know, like, how can this be true, what you're saying?"

"How could she think that I would be amenable to her, her way of thinking when her—just the way she was treating me was just degrading.

"She's not the girl I raised. She's not—she's not the daughter that I knew. She's a completely different person. She's just not Christie, to me, she's not Christie.

"She abandoned her family. She turned her back on us, fully turned her back on us. Completely. She knows what she's doing. She absolutely knows what she's doing. And she has only herself to blame."

Christie Rinder's Mother

This is what happens to people that get sucked into the noise, Christie fell for it and look where she is today. She is hanging out with the reality of what it is like to not have hope, help, purpose, friends, and family – which are the consequences to their actions.

When her father spoke about the incident, this is what he had to say about it:

"Christie made the decision to leave us if we didn't do what she wanted. But, you know, after all this time and all she's said and all she's done, it's like, she's not a loving daughter.

"Christie calls and talks to Liz [mother] and Christie starts sort of yelling and screaming at Liz, saying that she's a dupe. And that she's just been fooled and this—and that Christie has the straight data. And she's being vicious. Just being—I mean, neither Liz nor I had ever, ever, ever seen the viciousness that was displayed at this moment—ever, never, I'd never seen it. And it was like, "Wow, here she is doing that." And, I mean, I thought it was horrible.

"And I can remember telling my other children about it and they went, "She did that to Mom? She treated Mom like that?" Nobody could believe it. It would be like, "You're lying." I said, "No, I'm not lying. That's what she did." It was so unbelievably, horribly disgusting.

"What daughter treats a mom like that? Geez, it's hard to even find one in literature. You know, it's hard to find one in history. It's like nuts. People that are nuts, people that are wallowing around in the mire, that have lost their way and don't have

anything better to do than sort of strike out and lash out.

"And I mean you lash out at the person who loved you the most. In the whole wide world, the person who loved her the most was her mom, clearly without a—and here she is lashing out at her, publicly trying to humiliate her, just treating her like—horrible. And so, yeah, a person who could do that, oh my goodness, that's as low as it gets, isn't it? That's just terrible.

"For her to go on TV and denounce me and especially my wife was unthinkable. And we cared for her. We loved her. We were willing to do anything for her, but she says that we broke with her. Nah, we didn't break with her. She wanted me to do something really, really stupid and it wasn't going to happen. It wasn't going to happen at all. She broke with me."
Christie Rinder's Father

The fact that she switched that fast from false information is crazy. Did you know that could be the effect of false information? Whew!

Disconnection was not done by the mother and father; it was done by Christie herself.

MIKE RINDER, A PROFILE

I thought I would sum up the information you have gathered from this book about Mike Rinder in this profile.

Have you ever felt so cowardly that you ran away from responsibility? Have you ever felt so cowardly that taking responsibility was in the way of a great relationship with your family?

Scientology does not have anything to do with his cowardice. He has had this even before Scientology, according to many sources.

Rinder joined the Sea Organization, Scientology's religious order, as he found that it worked for him and worked for others.

There are things that Rinder tries to hide from his unstable follower base. There are statements he has made about Scientology helping others.

Scientology has helped millions of individuals. Rinder knows this, even if he was not a good legal director, it is hard to ignore the successes when they happen daily. Members of the Church are very vocal about their experiences, and they want to share them with everyone, this includes those who are in higher positions of the religion. The people in higher positions of the religion want to hear about these successes because this is what they are doing their duties for – to continue these successes. These happen in front of those working with religious officials, including a legal director as he has been entrusted to handle these functions to the best of his ability and beyond.

Rinder tends to try to ignore the statements he has made in his past, as he has already confessed the following about the testimonies he has provided while in the Church:

"Question: It wasn't always your practice to present the truth to

courts in affidavits and declarations, was it, sir?

"Rinder: Of course, it was."

(Deposition)

Which means, everything that will be presented in this profile is true coming from Rinder. The unstable will try to make up why it is not true and why it should not be true and all the illogical points we have no interest in when we are talking about cold-hard facts, so ignore the noise and let us confront reality.

"The tactic is as transparent as it is unconscionable—spread venom in the hope that the victims of the hate campaign will eventually be forced to buy their silence so the Church can get on with its real purpose of expanding the Scientology religion and helping more people."
Mike Rinder, Affidavit

To fully understand this statement, one must understand the examples of this in action.

The Church is fundraising for a building in Ketchikan, Alaska, and Rinder finds out about it. He tries *everything* including going on the news to spread some false information that is "alarming" and then causes some in the community to believe it because it sounds "real" and is posed as "we need to take action now". What does he want the Church to do in response to this? Buy him off. He wants the Church to call *him* and give him whatever he asks for in return for his silence on the false information. He knows the Church is getting on with expansion and helping people without stopping his rumormongering campaign.

Rinder also uses this tactic to get the Church to settle in court, he coaches the witnesses, helps the attorneys manufacture the testimonies to fit the case. In Rinder's fantasy world, the Church would have no say in anything as he would have made the judge and the jury believe that Scientology is going to use some canceled policy from the 1960's that has been misinterpreted, which he has confirmed on TV.

The policy has been altered by Rinder and his cohorts to mean something else and is now being used, *not* in Scientology, but in their Anti-Scientology Cult.

The truth is wild and crazy. I did not believe it when I first researched it and then to find affidavits that verified my view, I knew it was the truth. I knew Rinder and his cohorts were trying to project it onto Scientology and Scientologists so extortion would work more effectively, as well as framing Scientologists for their crimes.

One of the main points he has been trying to project is that he *did* beat his ex-wife that night in Clearwater, Florida. There is evidence and testimony of this occurring. Rinder has tried his hardest to ensure that this didn't get out into the public.

"Mike Rinder physically attacked me and caused permanent damage to my shoulder over 5 years ago. His attack resulted in my going through surgery and subsequent years of physical rehabilitation. I have pain every day of my life and have a crippled shoulder. Mike Rinder not only attacked me but has a history of violence to women. It's all been documented."
Cathy Bernardini

It all started when Rinder abandoned his family and his Church in 2008 when British Broadcasting Corporation (BBC) visited the Church of Scientology in Sussex, UK. Rinder was disgruntled about his demotion due to his illegal activities and that Scientology was investigating every activity he was guilty of. He ran away and visited BBC to sign a contract with them.

Before abandoning his wife and his kids, he was given a position as the Church Spokesperson's personal assistant. He was the errand boy. He was delivering hot coffee, lunch, snacks, and anything else that was requested by Mr. Tommy Davis of the Church of Scientology International to help fulfill the position.

"I was married to Mike Rinder for over 30 years. Mike deserted me, our children, and his entire family on 10 June 2007. He walked out, left without a word and did it knowing what he was doing. He disconnected from each and every one of us knowingly and without any remorse. After spending most of our lives together he walked out on his family, his friends, and his career."

Cathy Bernardini

Honestly, what Rinder did was horrific, and his lack of responsibility shows just how cowardice he has become.

That is all I will state on this subject as you can do your own research on the 'Justice4Mom' website where there is a multitude of documents, videos, and articles on this.

THE BACKPAGE CONNECTION

Ever wonder where the talk about human trafficking comes from with Mike Rinder and his posse? Using the projection data in the last chapter, you should know that there is a reason for this.

Remember the mention of Tony Ortega being his cohort? What has Ortega done?

"The people I work for were smart enough to start Backpage.com."

Tony Ortega, 2011

"Federal authorities have taken down Backpage.com, a major classified advertising website that has been repeatedly accused of

enabling *prostitution and sex trafficking of minors.* "

New York Times

This is very serious. But what does this have to do with the Anti-Scientology Cult and Rinder? What does this have to do with the research I have done into the ASC?

Tony Ortega is the man behind Mike Rinder, Leah Remini, and the rest of the ASC's "public relations". He is the man you will find in the closet, in a coffee shop, sitting on someone's couch, and even lurking near the bushes on his laptop inventing some cover-ups for his cohorts.

Why do we care to address Ortega?

The Truth

Ortega was an editor at the Village Voice which was linked to the Backpage website. Apparently, Village Voice was getting their funding from Backpage.

The executives of the Voice were very concerned that they would be held responsible for the fallout of Backpage. But, since Backpage was funding the Voice's operations and managed their financials – they had to defend it.

A CNN reporter did a full investigation into Backpage and exposed the operation. This investigation opened the public's eyes to the trafficking that was going on and the truth behind the slimy website.

What was Ortega's response to this investigation? He attacked the respected reporter by stating the network is junk science and a culmination of mass paranoia. This was stated as an editor of the Village Voice and as an attempt to make him look good to his bosses.

He was not done there, he also stated that CNN's report on Backpage was a sensationalistic piece, that it was manipulative, and had something to do with a semi religious crusade.

If you read the CNN report on Backpage's actual activities, it is none of the above stated by Ortega. Which makes me wonder, how much did he get paid for this piece? Why was this not blasted throughout the media verse?

But Ortega was known for his attempts at covering up his crimes with Backpage and Village Voice. He must have been feeling the heat from the Church of Scientology's investigations into his dealings, the CNN report, and the public looking at the Village Voice and Backpage's operations.

"Tony Ortega takes two teenagers, already brutally raped by thugs, and editorially sodomizes them by appropriating their identities, putting lies in their mouths, and pimping them as shameless opportunists who would do anything for a buck. Then he writes another fabrication claiming the fictional reporter was fired."

The Daily Cannibal

The fact that The Daily Cannibal released this about Ortega pushes me in the direction of pressure. There must have been a lot of pressure coming from the bosses of Ortega and mostly due to his actions on Backpage.

We are talking about Ortega who had a hand in editing the listings on Backpage to adjust them to not get caught by the Feds and to still offer teenagers for sexual use. He was using them as objects through the editing of these listings to make it easier for them to be sold to others without being stopped or tracked.

He is ruthless when it comes to cover-ups for himself and his cohorts. This explains so much about this man. He is a monster and should not be permitted to live without justice being served for his hand in sex and human trafficking.

The FBI would have a field day with this information if he were not given a payday to leave and not say a word about the Backpage and the Voice connection and the work he did for them. But there are fortunately articles everywhere about Backpage and the Voice being part of this so that we can expose the operation in its entirety even without Ortega's piece (for now).

What is very interesting about Ortega is that he was fired from the Voice but, it is not for the reason(s) you might think he was fired for.

"He flew all the way down to South Texas, to my home, and he had just got fired from the Village Voice, which he sort of converted into this anti-Scientology platform for two years.

"And, at a rare moment where he had a motive to be somewhat candid, he told me about the circumstances on which he left the Village Voice and the circumstances he said, this can't go anywhere but what happened was that the Village Voice had been accused and factually been investigated by law enforcement of human trafficking and promoting the child sex slave industry by its Backpage's ads.

"He told me that, you know, Scientology had been exposing that he said the problem is, is that Scientology was more accurate than anybody thought. And, that in fact the Village Voice was almost exclusively financed by that human trafficking operation and that there were profits beyond that. So, the owners, now that Scientology was exposing it and law enforcement was investigating it, decided they had to get rid of Tony Ortega because he was just obsessed with Scientology and he was keeping their focus on him and their operation, so they needed to get rid of him.

"In order to do that and extract his cooperation in keeping quiet about what he knew, which is interesting because of course he is

the first one to accuse anybody who doesn't go after Scientology as being bought off, right.

"He literally agreed to cover it up and obstruct justice for a payout of essentially a two-year buyout deal. They paid him enough to where he could literally do nothing for two years and go out and write a book on Scientology so he could begin with some foundation of credibility upon which to continue his career which he had turned into trashing Scientology."

Mark Rathbun, Former "Guru" to Leah Remini

This tells me a lot about Ortega. This tells me that he is dishonest, a criminal, and a coward. He could not face the fact that he needed to step forward and take responsibility for what he had done to those teenagers on the website.

This also shows me that Leah Remini, Mike Rinder, Amy Scobee, and the rest of the Anti-Scientology Cult members have no problem brushing this under the rug and continuing to project this onto Scientology, as if their former religion had something to do with this operation.

These people are sick. They are willing to sweep this entire operation under the rug because of their hate of being caught in the Church and their vengeance against Mr. David Miscavige that they are willing to push these victims to the side for a witch hunt. This is insanity. They think it is acceptable to sweep obstruction of justice and a Backpage cover-up aside and continue with their agendas.

Why does this make me feel so sick inside? Why didn't Remini and Rinder share this on their show?

The cover-up is so real that it is sickening. These individuals want to project "no responsibility" onto Scientology but, it is the ASC. Ortega is the PR Representative for the ASC and is one of Leah and Mike's trusted friends. They have been everywhere together and done all their crimes together.

I will not stop until Ortega is behind bars with his bosses. I will involve all the authorities until this is sorted out. These teenagers deserve justice and since Ortega was part of it – that is exactly what I will do.

If you would like to join the movement in ensuring justice is served, reach out to me on social media and let us create some motion towards justice.

AFFIDAVIT OF
MIKE RINDER

This was typed word for word based off the hard copy affidavit. This is worth your attention as you will find him contradicting these statements, brushing them aside, and pretending like he never said them. Please note that he verified that these are factual statements by deposition in 2015.

UNITED STATES DISTRICT COURT
FOR THE CENTRAL DISTRICT OF CALIFORNIA
CASE NO. CV 91-6426 HLH(Tx)

CHURCH OF SCIENTOLOGY INTERNATIONAL
a California Non-Profit Religious Organization,

DECLARATION OF MICHAEL RINDER
     Plaintiff,

  vs.

    STEVEN FISHMAN AND UWE GEERTZ,
    Defendants.

I, Michael Rinder, hereby declare and state:

1. I am a Director of the Church of Scientology International (CSI). I was raised in the Scientology religion and have been a staff member in the Church since 1973. As such, I have personal knowledge of the facts set forth in this declaration and if called as a witness, I could and would testify

completely thereto.

2. As a Director of CSI, I have seen the filings made by the defendants and their lawyers in this case over the past six months.

3. Clearly, the focus of the defendants has not been on trying to disprove the defamation of which they were guilty or even to address issues related to the defamation. Instead, they have sought to turn this case into a witch hunt of the Scientology religion. In doing so, the paid witnesses have specifically targeted the leader of the religion, David Miscavige, for their abusive lies and outrageous accusations.

4. Why would defendants and their counsel devote such an inordinate amount of attention to a non-party such as David Miscavige? Why would defendants' counsel's mercenary witness expose their lack of credibility so plainly by their resort to such outrageous and false allegations about him when he never had any involvement with Fishman, Geertz, or this case? It is apparent that their effort to denigrate the leader of the religion is part of a campaign to create a false impression of, and thereby, denigrate Scientology. The lies that have been propagated in this case are vile beyond description. Their purpose, as made clear by Graham Berry himself, is to use them as a threat to extort funds from the Church. They have gotten away with this barrage of lies so far, and as a consequence, Berry now has the precedent of this case to use to create a future threat that he hopes will prompt CSI to pay to make him take his lies and go away.

5. David Miscavige prevented the Aznarans and Youngs from carrying out what would have been a catastrophic turn of events for the religion. Vicki Aznaran and Vaughn Young were involved in a scheme to pervert the scriptures of L. Ron Hubbard for their own profit. They were caught and stopped by David Miscavige. For this, every Scientologist is grateful. Even

then, they were given the opportunity to redeem themselves within the Church. While they now rail against Mr. Miscavige and unleash the foulest lies about him their imaginations can concoct, any Scientologist would have thought it totally proper under the circumstances for those people to have been expelled from the Church without a chance for mercy. However, he gave them another chance. I know that he personally spent many hours with both Vicki Aznaran and Vaughn Young trying to help them regain their self-respect. They decided that rather than face those whom they had betrayed, that they would leave staff. Mr. Miscavige even helped the Aznarans to get themselves established in a new job. They were encouraged to continue in Scientology and treated civilly, as even they have testified elsewhere. Yet, all this being true, the Youngs and Aznarans still have deep-seated hatred for Mr. Miscavige and have used this litigation to vent that hatred and to seek millions of dollars for their silence. There is no justifiable explanation for this, just as there is no explanation for savages dismembering missionaries who work for years helping them overcome poverty and disease. One can seek to help others and treat people with compassion and dignity, but the blind hatred harbored by a few cannot be restrained, no matter how hard one might try.

6. These people have gathered around them a few others who are bitter and harbor an unabiding resentment of Scientology and what it stands for and for their own failures in the Church. They view the Church as their "lottery ticket" and pursue their jackpot with lies and threats at the expense of the millions of happy and satisfied members who support the Church with their time and donations. The Aznarans and Youngs are joined in that pursuit by the likes of Hana Whitfield, Andre and Mary Tabayoyon, Larry Wollersheim, Steve Fishman, and Gerry Armstrong. Though they either do not know David Miscavige, or had some remote contact with him many years ago, they are willing to make vindictive allegations, not based on personal knowledge or the truth, and defame him personally and as the

leader of the religion. The tactic is as transparent as it is unconscionable – spread venom in the hope that the victims of the hate campaign will eventually be forced to buy their silence so the Church can get on with its real purpose of expanding the Scientology religion and helping more people.

7. While these so-called experts have no personal knowledge concerning David Miscavige, I do. I have known and worked with him since 1976.

8. The sheer volume of despicable allegations made about him are intended to create the false impression that where there is smoke there is fire. These "witnesses" know only too well from their experience in the Church that the tactic of telling bigger and bolder lies has been a strategy employed against the Church in litigation for years. Tell enough lies, and make enough allegations, and an impression will be created which accomplishes the end of destroying a reputation no matter how untrue the allegations are. Public figures are especially susceptible to this fraud as any study of history shows. Jesus Christ was crucified based on the false accusations of Judas Iscariot and the prejudice of the Romans.

9. Pontius Pilate listened to the lies about Jesus and the Christians. The Germans bought the lies about the Jews. Innocence does not prevent the lies from being told. And when those lies fall on ears opened by bigotry and deaf to the truth, irreparable harm is done. Defendants' tactics in this case are a study in this technique.

10. I know David Miscavige personally. As such I know him to be completely honest, and sincerely dedicated to helping people. For what he has done to expand our religion, he has the respect and admiration of millions of Scientologists. And for this same reason, he has earned the enmity and particular scorn of those with a vendetta against Scientology.

11. In the last decade, he has personally done more to ensure Scientology is standardly applied and made more widely known and available than any other single individual. After L. Ron Hubbard, the Founder of Scientology, passed away in 1986, the religion entered a new phase. While there will never be another L. Ron Hubbard, his death marked a time of potential disruption and upheaval, and Mr. Miscavige shouldered the responsibility for not only keeping the scriptures pure, but for guiding our religion into a time of great stability and rapid growth. He never sought personal power or aggrandizement; he was thrust into the position he currently holds precisely because he is so dedicated to helping others through our religion. It is because he has demonstrated time and time again his integrity and selfless willingness to serve for the good of others that he enjoys the support of the staff and parishioners of the Scientology religion.

12. I have spoken to him often, and spent a considerable amount of time working with him on various matters from the positions I have held throughout the years. I know from my own observation that he works sixteen hours a day, seven days a week without respite for only reason – his sincere dedication to bettering the lives of others. He and his wife live in a single motel-style room. He eats with the rest of the staff in the communal dining room, he drives his own car and carries his own bags. He regularly partakes in general group activities. It would shock most people that anyone would work so hard for so little material reward. It certainly gave pause to ABC News when they saw it with their own eyes.

13. Until 1981, David worked, like hundreds of other Church staff, in positions that dealt with the internal operations of the religion. Apart from the staff he dealt with directly as part of his duties, few knew who he was. I never heard an unkind word said about him. That changed when he took action to protect the future of the Church by taking over and disbanding

the Guardian's Office. This story has been recounted before, but there are three things about it that bear repetition. First, what he did took an enormous amount of courage, for with no authority other than the moral authority of someone dedicated to the well-being of our Church, he overthrew what was at the time the most feared and powerful group in Scientology (that they were feared is exactly why they had gone so far in contravention of Church policy as they were only answerable to themselves). Second, even after having achieved this feat, he did not seek a high profile position or attempt to "take over" the Church. He was happy to have those who were charged with running the Church continue to do so and have no part of it. Third, the overthrow of the Guardian's Office began what I have seen to be a virtually unending history of personal attacks against him. He didn't change, he merely became a known name and high-profile target.

14. Over the last thirteen years, I have seen a parade of personal attacks leveled at Mr. Miscavige which would have caused a less determined and less capable individual to give up and relinquish the position of "lightning rod" for anyone seeking to disrupt or destroy the Church. The first years saw attacks by government agencies, since proven totally false and unfounded, and documented by the government's own files gained through the Freedom of Information Act. These attacks went on for more than a decade. Government agencies amassed a huge volumes of files on him personally, and were aided by civil litigants who also jumped on the bandwagon and targeted Mr. Miscavige with their spite and malevolence. And in the face of this, when it would have been so easy to give up and walk away, never to be vilified or attacked again, I have seen him persist, because what he was doing in Scientology is important and invaluable to all those who are helped by L. Ron Hubbard's technology. That determination was buttressed by the fact that none of the accusations made about him were true.

15. Mr. Miscavige is very approachable and friendly. He gives regular briefings to Scientology parishioners and staff in our Churches around the world. I estimate that he does such public briefings about 35 times a year. He stops and talks with the staff and public everywhere he goes. I have been with him on many occasions where he has stayed until the early morning hours to talk to individuals who remained after one of his briefings. It is remarkable how many people know him and approach him as a friend. Thousands write to him to request his assistance on a wide variety of topics, and he always takes the time to help or see that help is gotten.

16. It is David Miscavige who has been the driving force in getting every single book, and all materials of the Scientology Grade Chart, fully and strictly in accordance with the writings of L. Ron Hubbard. Every Scientologist is eternally thankful for this because it means the full availability of the complete Scientology scriptures as written or spoken by Mr. Hubbard. He took no credit for this accomplishment, though those of us who are aware of the enormous amount of time he spent working to make this goal a reality know that the credit he so graciously gave to others, in fact, belonged to him.

17. Perhaps less important in his eyes than what he does internally in the Church, he has directly and personally given a new face to Scientology through his appearances in the media, responding eloquently and effectively to the same, discredited allegations that have been again dragged into this case.

18. And it is also David Miscavige who made the tax exemption by the IRS possible. It is he who personally walked into the front lobby of the IRS National Headquarters and through two years of persistent work,

ultimately brought about a peace with the IRS that had seemed impossible. But perhaps the most telling point is this: it was the IRS targeting individual Scientologists, merely because they were Scientologists, that motivated him the most in this endeavor. Again, he didn't take credit for this, he has told me many times that he felt it was his duty to all Scientologists to carry this off so they would be free to practice their religion just like those of other faiths.

19. I have observed through the years David's dedication to helping his fellow staff in the Church. It is he who raised the standards and conditions for staff members by insisting on constantly upgraded living quarters, dining areas and other staff facilities. It is he who has insisted on staff enhancement programs, and recreational facilities being provided for the staff of the Church. Absurd allegations of slave labor being employed in the Church turn my stomach. I know the truth. They are lies, and those who utter them know them to be lies.

20. Mr. Miscavige has been the driving force in establishing the ideal school where my children have an environment free from drugs and crime. My children and their peers know him as a friend and think the world of him for his thoughtfulness and care for their well-being and their education.

21. I know his compassion from personal experience. While Vicki Aznaran makes cruel claims concerning the death of my infant daughter, she does not know what in fact occurred, or if she does, she is simply lying to try to create a false impression. In this time of great personal upset, David and his wife Shelly supported my wife and me beyond what could possibly be expected by anyone – seeing to our personal needs, arranging for the most highly trained auditors to give us spiritual counselling (counseling), arranging plane fares and reservations, helping with the

funeral arrangements and making it as easy as possible in every fashion imaginable for us to come through this upsetting time. I resent any implication that has been made to the contrary by Vicki Aznaran – her statements are beneath contempt.

22. On many occasions I have seen David go out of his way to help others. I well recall two times where I took ill and it was David who called the doctor and personally ensured that everything possible was done to help me recover. He contacted the doctor (both occasions were late at night and required tracking down doctors in the middle of the night) and ensured I was properly treated. It would have been easy for him to let someone else take care of me, but he did so personally, and would not leave or rest until the matter was resolved. These are things I will never forget.

23. I have seen him act in a similar fashion with many others. As I work with him often, and know many of the people that know him, I am aware of the high regard in which he is held by Scientologists and those he comes in contact with. I have never heard a negative statement made about him by anyone other than those who seek to extort money from the Church. It really is that simple.

24. Comparing what I know to what I read in the declarations of these paid "witnesses", makes the lies even more vivid and callous. There is no resemblance to the individual I know that can be drawn from the innuendo, allegations and falsehoods that are written about him. To believe the statements of this tiny handful of spiteful apostates, in the face of such overwhelming evidence to the contrary, would be to listen to the testimony of Judas Iscariot. Their lies are no less bold, baldfaced or malicious.

I declare under penalty of perjury under the laws of the United States of America that the foregoing is true and correct.

Executed this 11th day of April, 1994.

Signed,
Michael Rinder

ANDREW RINDER, MIKE'S BROTHER

You know, we were so opposites in personality, beingness and intention, we grew apart very quickly. Fortunately, I grew bigger than him even though I'm younger than him and that was about the only protection I had. It's interesting that at the age of about 10 months old he tried to kill me with stuffing bread down my throat, so I choked. But I just couldn't ever get to actually like him. That's sad but true.

Mike—his intention was what was good for Mike. That's not the viewpoint of a Scientologist at all. The subject of Scientology is about the willingness to serve and help others. And really even now he's just a parasite to the subject and I don't think he ever, ever duplicated or got the idea of what Scientology really is. His only claim to fame is that he was a part of it. But was he ever really a part of it? No. He served, but he was never really an understanding person. So, you know, from day one he never got it.

The fact that he claims that we don't want to have any dialogue with him is a joke, because the truth is he doesn't want to have any dialogue with us except for a sensationalist idea or viewpoint. He has no interest in us whatsoever, and the truth is I don't have an interest in him either. Never have done.

He did say he would be willing to talk to me. But it was so ridiculously insincere it was amazing. His idea was that he could "turn" me. Turn me to what? Turn me from what? Come on, what is this, some alien movie or something? So yes, he did try and drive away. Yes, he just about cracked my finger. And he definitely damaged Cathy's shoulder which is a permanent situation. It was not pleasant. I went to see if I could help him, but he is beyond help.

I would never want to talk to him, because my life as a Scientologist is what I do. His is the total opposite. He is denigrating everything I do, my family does, my children, our future. It's like well, thanks very much but no thanks.

He's a parasite. Mike today is just a parasite, living off his past so-called experience. That's all he is. He doesn't create or do anything of decency. He has no kindness. There's not an inch of kindness in that body.

I look at Mike and I actually—I don't even have any pity anymore because he continues. So, to me he is just a lost loser, and I don't see any idea of how his life will continue to be, unless he can be a so-called expert. There is nothing else he has.

I can't even work out what it is that he's claiming to be an expert on. "All right, you think you know about Scientology. Well, if you do, what are you doing to help?" All he is doing is destruction and living off a hate or a fear or an inferiority within himself. There is no constructive decency in what he's doing at all.

BEN RINDER,
MIKE'S SON

I was diagnosed with cancer and that's a rough time for someone especially—I mean, you sit down in a room with five or six doctors, and they diagnosed you that you need to make some serious decisions about your life right now, because in five years you're not going to be alive. And to sit in a room and then have to think about that and think about the decisions and then not have like a father figure there for you is—I find it maybe selfish on his—maybe I'm selfish, but selfish on his part that there's absolutely nothing like your child is literally told he's going to be dead in five years. Nothing. So nonetheless I dealt with that, and we figured out and did a lot of research and my mom and sister researched a lot. I went through the whole procedure, and it's been eight, seven, eight years and I'm not dead and I think I can attribute that to my group. And actually, recovered better than I should have, and he wasn't there for it at all.

So, during my cancer treatment, the whole cycle from beginning to end, he did not contact me once. He didn't offer to help pay the medical bills; he didn't maybe ensure that I was getting the best treatment that we could get. He did nothing. He was not involved at all. So, I could have died. He wouldn't have even known.

I was in the sauna and two policemen came into the sauna, "We need to see you." So, I got up, went out of the sauna. Basically, said your dad is at the front of the building and he wants to see you, he's waiting for you. And for a moment you can think "Oh maybe there's a bit of compassion there" or care. But then you think "Well wait a sec, what's the only reason he would be standing in front of the Fort Harrison with a camera crew trying to come and get me, getting the police involved?" He is just trying to make himself right maybe or prove a point like "look how bad they treated us" and to create a fabricated story or something. And I said "I want nothing to do with him, I don't want to talk to him, I don't want to see him. I want nothing to do with him. I'm living my life and I'm figuring it out, and he can live his life and he's on his own with that. I want nothing to do with it." And they said, "Okay. So, you want nothing to do with him?" "I want nothing to do with him."

He doesn't care about me, he doesn't. If I had died five years ago, it would have just been like "Shoot—I need another angle now to cause trouble or whatever." I'm perfectly happy with him not knowing anything about me. I don't care. I don't live my life trying to prove something. Doesn't matter to me.

It's absolutely a stunt, for sure. If he cared about me, he would have shown that maybe 25 years ago or 20 years ago or whatever. It was definitely a stunt.

When he left, he didn't contact me once. Other than showing up at the front of the Fort Harrison, he has never contacted me. I don't think he's ever called me in my life. Like I'm not talking about just since he left, I'm saying I don't think he has ever called me.

He's totally separated himself from us and we are all in touch. We are all doing what we've been doing, moving on with life.
We were all in the same space. Like here's all of us in this circle. We are all still here except for him. He's the only one that moved out of this hypothetical space. I think that defines disconnection. We're all doing exactly what we were doing, what we've always been doing. We're doing better and we're totally fine. And I think he's the odd one out.

CATHY BERNARDINI, MIKE'S EX-WIFE

Most of my adult life I was with Mike Rinder. And in 2007 he went to the UK— he went off to England for a work-related trip and he didn't return on the day he was expected. I didn't hear anything from him at all and tried to contact him, because he didn't show up and couldn't find him. So, I of course was concerned that something had happened to him, or he was sick or something like that. And then days went by, didn't know where he was, didn't hear anything. And ultimately, like within the next week, he made contact with another person who's an associate of mine but not a family member or friend, even a close friend, to inform them that he wasn't coming back and that he had left.

There was no direct phone call to me. He could have picked up the phone and called me easily or an email directly to me or any communication to me or anything. It was just—I think the email was literally three lines long. There was nothing in it other than, "I'm leaving. Do you want—ask Cathy if she wants to come. Send me my stuff."

When we did finally get to see Mike, despite what he was purporting—that he wanted to be in communication with us and that we were not communicating when it was him that was not communicating— he was not happy to see us. The look on his face became one of hatred. It was really strange and like "Wow, what's happening here?" He was not happy to see us.

All of a sudden it was like he turned into an animal. He suddenly—it was in a split second and it was shocking to me—in a split second he suddenly changed and started growling at me. At the same time, he grabbed my arms and crisscrossed them in front of me and had his thumbs stuck particularly in my right forearm and had his car keys. And he's quite large compared to me and his hands absolutely engulf my arm, and he's very strong. And my instinct was to move, and every time I tried to move—Mike tightened the grip every time I tried to move and then was pushing my, pulling my arms down as if to sort of push them against my body so I also couldn't move my legs. And I was screaming to stop. And he put his face right up against me and he was like this—rrr, like this, and he stuck his eyes right up to my eyes. And he was so hateful, it was evil, vicious. And it was as if he was letting it all out all of a sudden, what he really always probably felt and wanted to make sure that I got how much he hated me and he wanted to hurt me.

I really couldn't move my arm after that for quite some time. Had extensive physical therapy for two years, which slowly I was able to regain movement starting with my hand and working up my arm. And at this point in time, I am in pain every day. It goes in degrees from worst to best and I still am doing various handlings on it every day so that I keep the circulation going and so I don't have as much pain. But I won't apparently regain full use of my shoulder or that arm. So, I am what they term "functional."

The true Mike Rinder is the one that when his own child, his brother and his wife come graciously to meet with him to communicate, he turned on me and turned into a wild animal and attacked me and permanently damaged my shoulder and my arm; tried to hurt his brother; then takes his girlfriend to break into his own mother's residence to paw through her stuff—for whatever reason I don't even know—photograph it and even give that data to the press, is so unbelievable and so not normal. It's that Mike Rinder. That is part of Mike's modus operandi. That is what his apparency is and under that there's some other agenda and some other way he's thinking how he's going to get you, how this is, as long as it benefits him, then that's the way it is. He'll say, he'll do anything if it benefits him.

He doesn't care. He doesn't care about his own mother.

He is obviously making up stories and lying beyond anything you could ever imagine to the point where he's weaving a web of delusion and has convinced himself of this too. It's like someone you find in an institution that's living in their own world, when in the real world actually the facts are so totally different you can't even imagine how did they come up with this. That's Mike Rinder.

TARYN TEUTSCH, MIKE'S DAUGHTER

As a dad, I wouldn't really call him a dad. Just by the fact that a dad is someone that you depend on, that is there with you, that lives your life with you, that goes through your special, your good, your bad and all of that and I wouldn't say that he held that function or did any of those things for me and even more so for my brother.

Before that he wasn't in my life at all. When I was 8 years old, I got hit by a car. It was a hit and run and I almost, I almost died. I mean they thought I might die. And if you ask me right now, I can't—I don't remember my dad ever being there, ever, ever, ever. Not once. I have no recollection of even seeing him or—I'm trying—you know I thought about it recently and I was like, "Wow, I don't think he was ever there." Not once, but my mom was there every single day.

Because of the way he treated me and because of those non-gestures by an early, my early teens or late teens I thought he hated me. Like, I was positive.

He never said goodbye, he never gave us a letter, he never said, "Okay kids, I'm off, you can have your choice." Nothing.

I went there with my mom and my uncle thinking, "Okay good, let's go see him and give him the benefit of the doubt and see if we can reconcile this, once and for all. He can go on his own way, I'm totally fine with that like—but just stop attacking me and saying things about me or my family or my family members." Okay good, we go to see him. First of all, I would say outright, I was, I was shocked at how bad he looked. Like meaning, when I saw him, I was like, "Whoa. He looks whacked, he looks crazy to me, and his eyes looked funny." I mean, it was just—I hadn't seen him and then I saw him, and I was like, "Wow, oh my god. That's, that's Mike." And my mom was there, and she was speaking to him and at one point he totally and utterly lost it.

He was—you could tell his only interest in the conversation was getting something the media could use because he was like, "I'm getting the BBC on the phone" or whatever. So, he was all frantic about that and crazy. He didn't even, he wouldn't even listen. He wouldn't even have a conversation and go, "Wow, my kid's here, my wife's here, my brother's here, they all came to see me, why don't I stop a minute and hear what they have to say." No, he wouldn't listen to us, he then grabbed my mom's arm and I guess there was a key or something he had in his hand, his car key and he's grabbing her arm so bad, she's going, "Ow, ow, ow, ow! Stop, Mike stop!" And he gouged her arm. But not only that but he actually—I don't know exactly, technically what he did, but he pulled her arm out, okay. So now it's years later, right now, as we're talking, 2016, and every day she's in pain, every single day. She had surgery and she'll never have proper function of it and… So, she's sitting there screaming and—this is his wife. I mean, he was still married to her at this time even though he decided to go with another woman but that's a whole 'nother story. And he's hurting her like, badly hurting her. She's a small woman, she's pretty frail, like meaning she has small bones and stuff, and he was squeezing her and, and she's going "Stop, stop! It's hurting." You know, and he's just like, "Yeah! No, it's not!" And I can't remember what he said but I think he was saying like, "Yeah right." I don't remember what he said but it wasn't very nice, but I do remember seeing the interaction between him and my mom. Mike Rinder and my mom. And I remember going, "Oh my god, he hates her." Like he was just like, "Grrr! Bitch!" Like really bad like, scary, I was like, "Wholly crap, that's my dad, doing that to my mom."

Mike's brother Andrew then tried to talk to him even more and was like, "Look man, just stop and talk to us." And he was just like, "I'm out of here!" and trying to get in his car and leaving and then he ends up basically like, bending my uncle's fingers back, completely hurting him. And refused to talk to us and just, I don't know, I went away from it, and I went, "Wow, there's something really wrong with him."

Even when he was with us, he treated everybody like shit. He treated us like, really like, like we were nothing. I'm telling you; you would have a conversation with him, you would walk away and go, "I suck." It was the way he made you feel that you were horrible, and this is coming from his daughter and his son, I mean my brother—he never liked him, he didn't like him.

My grandmother had quite a few times spoken up and or written to him saying, "Please stop, stop attacking my family, my church." Like, she is a founding Scientologist, her and my grandfather were. And so, they've put a lot of their own lives and love and their heart into creating this religion and forwarding it. So, he comes along and not only deserts his immediate family, meaning me, my brother and my mom, but her, his brother, his sister who are all also Scientologists, and their kids. So not only did he desert us, leave his mom which of course that's just like—he just left, never said anything to her either. Then he starts attacking the one thing that, you know, the thing she's put her heart into the most and our religion and our family and he starts attacking that.

So, she's saying, "Mike, please just—can you not do this? Can you please—I'm fine on you not being in Scientology, we're all okay on that. Go have your life, be with Jack and your wife, that's totally fine. We're happy with that." But he wouldn't stop and so she kept saying, "Can you please stop doing this, can you please just..." Okay, so then that incident happened where he went in her room. Shortly after that she got very ill, within probably I would say about a year. She got very ill and then she was on her deathbed, literally on her deathbed. We were getting calls from the hospital in Australia, like, "Okay, she's going to die any day now." And the last thing she asked is, "I wish Mike—I was on the phone with her—and she says, I wish Mike would come to his senses. I wish I didn't have a son that did this."

For him to say anything to Leah Remini in her show or otherwise—factually to anybody for that matter, especially people that—I don't know them at all. They've never experienced my life or my family's life and my childhood or what I went through or even now in the present the way that our family operates—which is amazing, the best ever. So, for Mike to now tell or to say on the show or to insinuate in any way that 1) he knows anything about me, or 2) that I or my brother or my mom disconnected from him is just a total farce. Like by true definition he's the one that disconnected.

My comment on him being a consultant for Leah Remini on the subject matter of disconnection specifically is actually a little bit laughable. Because as a consultant, you would think it would be someone that does whatever that thing is, that is a good example of whatever you're trying to show. And yet he is the exact opposite of that. So, he disconnects from his family. He leaves both of his kids. I don't remember how old I was at the time. But he never said goodbye, he never said anything. Left both of us in the lurch with no communication. Not one single piece of communication. Not an email, not a phone call, not a note, not a goodbye. Nothing. He left and never came back. So how does that person consult with, or become a consultant for that subject matter? I don't know. It doesn't make sense to me. That just seems absurd.

He fully and utterly misrepresents me, my lifestyle, my church, my friends, my mom, my brother, my family and everything having to do with it and does it knowingly—and does it to meet his own ends and so for me that signifies a liar.

Everyone in the family is just like, 'Wow, we didn't even realize how much, like what a black sheep he was," how much he put a little uuhhh on the family communication lines. And every single one of us has expanded and we're doing great, and we see each other more than ever. And I was just with Andrew and Pat last weekend. And my brother and Jackie and my cousin in Florida spent the weekend with Andrew and Pat a few weeks before that. And we went to New York, and we went to Australia. And we're going to go in December. Mike's sister and her family are coming. That didn't happen before. It just didn't happen. I don't remember ever seeing my family as much or see and feel our family as close as we are now, since he was removed, or removed himself from our family.

So, since he removed himself from our family, it's only gotten better and better. And everyone is just so much more vibrant and flourishing and prospering and doing well and more successful in their jobs. Like everything got better.

LIZ KING,
MIKE'S MOTHER-IN-LAW

My name is Liz King and I'm the mother of Christie—Christie Collbran Rinder, who I don't even know anymore, who is a stranger, a complete stranger to me.

She's totally nuts, she's not the girl I raised, she's not the daughter that I knew. She's a completely different person. She's just not Christie, to me. She's not Christie. And she chose to be that way, so she can't cry, she can't cry about losing her family. She turned her back on us, she turned her back on us and all of her friends.

Christie pretends in her statements that she's not responsible for what's occurred. But she has actually insulted me in the press and said degrading things about me in the press because I am a Scientologist. And her actions are insulting to my way of life. So, it seems to me what she's doing is she's pretending that she's being mistreated, but she's the one who has orchestrated all of this and made it happen.

All the things she says and all the things she does are all pretend and calculated to further her cause. She's trying to further her cause. And she's using me, she's using me and her family to do that, which to me is really low, incredibly low.

She absolutely knows that she's hurting me. She knows that she's hurting me, she knows that she's hurting her family, she knows that she's hurting her friends who she's abandoned, all of her friends. She knows that, but she just keeps going.

EDDIE KING, MIKE'S FATHER-IN-LAW

Christie calls and talks to Liz and Christie starts sort of yelling and screaming at Liz, saying that she's a dupe and that she's just being fooled, and that Christie has the straight data. And she's being vicious—neither Liz nor I had ever, ever, ever seen the viciousness that was displayed at this moment—ever, never, I'd never seen it. And it was like wow, here she is doing that, and I thought it was horrible. And I can remember telling my other children about it and they went "She did that to mom? She treated mom like that?" Nobody could believe it; it would be like "you're lying." I said, "No, I'm not lying, that's what she did." It was so unbelievably horribly disgusting.

What daughter treats a mom like that? It's hard to even find one in literature, it's hard to find one in history. It's like nuts, people that are nuts, people that are wallowing around in the mire, that have lost their way and don't have anything better to do than sort of strike out and lash out. And I mean, you lash out at the person who loves you the most? In the whole wide world, the person who loved her the most was her mom, clearly, and here she is, lashing out at her, publicly trying to humiliate her, just treating her like—horrible. And so yeah, a person who could do that, oh my goodness, that's as low as it gets, isn't it? That's just terrible.

For her to go on TV and denounce me, and especially my wife, was unthinkable. We cared for her, we loved her, we were willing to do anything for her, but she says that we broke with her. No, we didn't break with her. She wanted me to do something really, really stupid and it wasn't going to happen, it wasn't going to happen at all. She broke with me.

We had a great family, and we still have a really, really, really good family. We see my son twice a month and calls us if something is going wrong in his life, "Dad! Blah, blah, blah, blah." "Oh yeah? Well, this..." You know? We're tight, we are a good, close wonderful family and we all follow Scientology. Christie didn't have to follow Scientology if she didn't want to, but she couldn't just sort of dump on us or pull this kind of stuff. This isn't any part of being a good family, this isn't a part of being a loving daughter, this isn't part of being a good sister to her brother or her other sister. This is hater stuff, this is destructive.

I didn't see or hear too much more about her life, and what little teeny bit I heard would be like "Oh, my goodness." I heard that her ex-husband was doing drugs and he was doing this, and it was worse than that, and some of her friends that were now her friends, they were doing drugs. She came from an environment where nobody did drugs, not one person. We don't do drugs; we don't need drugs. Without drugs we are as happy as we can be. And she's with a group of people now that are using dope and marijuana and lord knows what else. So, I didn't have much more to do with her or hear too much more about her life.

GEORGINA TWEEDIE, MIKE'S FORMER COLLEAGUE

He had this air about him that he was the best professional, very trusted, he knew everything. But factually, it was a façade. There was no real person underneath that. There was nobody you could go talk to. There wasn't actual communication and interaction occurring, which is necessary in any business field, in any organization. It was just very difficult to work with him.

And what I found was, even though he was my direct boss, he was just ignoring me, basically. He would just sort of ignore me like I wasn't there. The only time we would interact would be at a meeting in the morning to do with the daily activities, and it was usually a very unpleasant meeting for myself and the other people from the other departments that were at that meeting. It was something that I couldn't wait till it was over each day—and dreaded, actually.

So, I would stand up and I would start to give some data about what was happening, and he would shoot me down in flames in front of 80 other staff members. I would just be in tears afterwards. Nothing I said was right. I was trying to very simply explain to everybody how search engines worked and what I was handling and what I was doing. It was beyond critical; it was just beyond critical. And it wasn't just me. This was being done with other staff members as well, and so watching it and watching other people in that position was very, very upsetting. It was extremely upsetting because it was like nobody could do anything right in his eyes.

And it's very hard to work with somebody that feels that way about you.

HANS SMITH, MIKE'S FORMER COLLEAGUE

In relation to Mike Rinder, I can say one thing which is, I've been working for the Church of Scientology for 24 years and in those 24 years I've worked in a lot of places. I've worked in England, I've worked in Europe, I've worked in Australia, I've worked in Asia, I've worked here in the United States, and I've met a lot of people, like thousands and thousands of people. And he's the only person in the last 24 years that I've been on staff who's punched me. He actually punched me in the chest once. Actually, he punched me so hard, I had a tag on, and he broke the tag in half. And that was—to me that's just the kind of person he is, just kind of an aggressive guy who honestly wasn't very popular. So that's just my personal experience with Mike Rinder.

He was just an unpleasant person. He wasn't somebody who was like "Oh, he's a good friend of mine." He never was friends with a lot of people because he just was, you know, an unpleasant person. I could say other words, but there are ladies and children who may watch this so shouldn't say them. But yeah. He was a...he was a jerk. That's how I would describe him.

JEFF BAKER, MIKE'S FORMER COLLEAGUE

Mike Rinder was into himself. He wasn't about helping other people. He was about him, actually, and that's not what a Scientologist is. It's a person who helps other people improve conditions in life, themselves, and other people. And Mike was about himself.

He was demeaning to people. He kind of looked down at them. He didn't work with them; he didn't work as a professional with them. He was a bit slighting, if you will, especially if something wasn't quite right. He wouldn't work to make it right; he would just comment that it wasn't or make somebody look bad because it was not right. And this was a typical thing for him.

I observed many times when something would mess up—you know, things don't always go exactly as planned—and if they didn't go as planned, his reaction to it wasn't to jump in and help, or get it sorted out, it was kind of like to laugh at it. In fact, he would laugh at it, at somebody's folly in messing something up. And he was not a team member to get something done.

Mike Rinder would go to events, and he was supposed to be there to talk about something that was his hat, that was his function. But because Mike Rinder never actually did anything, he would always come off like a wooden doll or a robot. He didn't speak from conviction or from the heart because he wasn't doing the activity that he was talking about. And you've seen when a speaker is convicted about something that they do, they know all about it, and it's theirs. It shows in their speech. They're not "doing a "speech," they're telling you something that really means something to them. Mike Rinder, when he'd get up, was like a wooden doll, because Mike Rinder never did what he was talking about. He was only talking about it. He was supposed to be doing something about it, but he never was. And that was the problem.

There were several times I observed personally, being in the room with him, while everyone is frantically working away to wrap up this video for our next event, and he's actually on the couch, in the edit bay, sleeping—while the whole event evolution is going on. Everyone else frantic, Mike sleeping. And that is actually commonly something that I would observe many times. We would have to wake him up to look at the video or even work on it. So that was kind of his attitude. He had a very lax attitude towards getting something done. And he certainly was not a hands-on person. He was a look-at and tell other people something to do, while he lounged on the couch, basically. And that is kind of typically what would happen.

I never saw him care personally for another individual. Mike mostly cared about himself. He was a bit into himself. In fact, not a bit, a lot into himself. And he wasn't a team member. He was almost an "addition" to the evolution that was going on. And sometimes a sleeping addition.

KATHY O'GORMAN, MIKE'S FORMER COLLEAGUE

I knew Mike Rinder and worked with him for 30 years, and this was probably 20, 25 years into our being colleagues. And what happened was he was told that a TV show was airing and when it was airing, and we went back to look at it because one of my staff members was in charge of taping the show. So, we go to tape the show, but it wasn't on, there was some mix-up on it or whatever. He went into a complete psychotic rage—he wasn't even aware where he was or anything. He took his clipboard and he just like went "whack," full body force into the side of my head—I think it was this side of my head—and it was just like psychotic. And it stung and in actual fact after the fact I found out that he actually broke my tooth. I wasn't even aware of it then because I was so shocked about what he had done that I just immediately... I just looked at him and I said something like "You're out of your mind."

No one had ever in my life, ever lifted a finger... to me. He's the only one that has ever taken a violent act against me. And that's Mike Rinder. And then I know that he's done this to others too. And the guy was completely psychotic!

Mike Rinder was a complete, total coward. He couldn't even confront up to his own actions much less—he took it out on women! Take it out on me?!

He tried to give the impression that he was on top of things or Mike Rinder was .... But he was actually really a lazy son of a bitch. And I let him know that then. It was like, he wouldn't look, he wouldn't inspect, he didn't even care what really happened.

MARCY MCSHANE, MIKE'S FORMER COLLEAGUE

Mike wasn't easy to work for. I guess an analogy I can give you that he was like a volcano about to erupt most of the time. He treated his staff like a tyrant. Not a lot of caring or true liking of a staff. It was always, in my view, a pretended, not real, caring for the staff. He was a tyrant, really.

I was squashed into a ball. It was oppressive working for him. It was hard. He didn't make it like a nice working relationship. It just wasn't like that.

There would be this vicious bent, a vicious strain in how he communicated. It's one thing to have a boss correct you, even firmly, about something, but there was this twist, this—I can say it's a vicious strain that was intertwined in his communication.

He used to frequently fall asleep at the desk. I frequently had to wake him up and tell him "Wake up, we have a deadline" or "We have something to get in" or "There's something imperative to get done." He had a habit of falling asleep at the desk, at the job.

I never in my life experienced physical abuse until I worked for Mike. He is vicious and he is a physical abuser. One time he forced me under a desk and then trapped me under the desk, he wouldn't let me out under the guise of fixing something or doing something. And he trapped me under there and then he was being lewd, like disgustingly lewd. And the more I clamored to get out from under there he wouldn't let me out. In fact, he called somebody and told them to get a camera so they could take a picture of me under the desk, and I was frantic. I didn't even know like what the heck he was doing. Then another time, I made some simple mistake. And I'm saying simple because what followed was nuts. I miswrote a communication or something. And he came over to me, gripped both my arms, tightly gripped my arms, and then started to shake me back with this wild, animal crazed look in his eyes. He was shaking me so hard my head was snapping back and forth and at that point I took my hands to cover my face because I thought he was going to hit me. And then he just pushed me, forced me, threw me into a wall. I, I didn't even understand what was happening, I, I didn't even get what warranted such behavior out of him, he, he was just crazed, just crazed.

There was a guy who, named Hans, who again made some error with a video product, or an A/V product and Mike picked him up and took him by, like, the neck and held him up against the wall and it took two other guys coming in and telling him, "No, hold on. Stop doing that. Knock it off, Mike." To get him to let go and let the guy - and this guy was big. But again, another reactive, reaction type and this same crazed, kind of like he's like not even there kind of thing happened at that time.

He has this vicious, attack, attack-type approach, and thing about him. It's like part of him. I don't think—I don't know. I just feel that that is, was his nature. It, it's like how he is. He's got, it's just this streak, this— vicious. Evil. And there's evilness in it as well. Like he wants to do harm, or he wanted to do harm, he wanted to create that effect.

LINDA HIGHT, MIKE'S FORMER COLLEAGUE

The 10 years that I worked with Mike Rinder were positively ghastly is about the nicest thing I can say about them. And for a staff member to say that about someone they worked for is so unusual, because the one thing that Scientology is known for internally and outside is our mutual respect for each other, our communication skills, our joy at doing a valuable job to the best of our ability. And Mike Rinder was the only person and remains the only person that I have ever encountered in this position who seemed to be utterly opposed and opposite to that way of operating.

Mike Rinder had a terrible time dealing with women in a professional setting. The thing that was peculiar about that was that it was 10 times worse for the women than it was for the men. It's not that he was pleasant to the men or complimented them, but it was very, very mild compared to the treatment that the women got in those meetings.

He picked on the women, and I don't mean just picked on them. I had a colleague who—I don't know how she survived it. And he even later once admitted in one moment of clarity that he had been very hard on her. That was about as far as he would go— "Yeah, I guess I was pretty hard on her." But he definitely dealt with women in a different way than he did with men. He was bad with all people, in my observation, but much, much worse with women.

There is no real Mike Rinder. Mike Rinder is like the Bermuda Triangle where you don't know which is the sky and which is the ocean and was he lying then, is he lying now? He doesn't know, he's got truth and fiction so mushed together in his morphing tales. If you watch his stories grow and change and evolve and I think, 'Wait a minute, that's not what he was saying before. Now he's saying that what in the-?' There is no truth with Mike Rinder. And that's one of the main reasons it was so confusing and so upsetting to work around him, because things were always different. It was like working on quicksand.

I think the only way to approach Mike Rinder is to assume that anything that comes out of his mouth is a lie. There would be no other way to deal with what he says. The only thing that I've ever read where I think he had a moment of some kind of self-revelation, that he probably backed away from very rapidly, was on some occasion before he left the Church, he wrote about himself. And he wrote about his own lying and how it didn't really matter to him if it was a lie or not and that he'd gotten so used to lying that he'd even lie about lying.

Mike Rinder is an utterly false person in my estimation. Everything about him is false—what he says, what he does, what he said and what he did. His estimation of other people was false, his estimation of himself was false. I think he built a false world around himself, and it only lasted until it didn't work anymore and then he was kicked out so he had to go out and build another false world. "False" is what I think of when I think of Mike Rinder—unable to carry on a civil conversation with any other human being, unable to say, "thank you," "good job," "I'm sorry," "you were right"—anything remotely like a decent human being would be.

He was just an underling but still keeping up this pretense of being an "executive" and being someone "important." This is the ultimate meritocracy in Scientology—you earn your position, and you keep your position by your merits, by what you do, not because of any other reason. But he was continually pushing himself as some super important person when he actually wasn't and was quite despised.

And it's simply another effort to make himself now—reinvent himself as something he never was. And if it weren't so serious and so offensive, it would be laughable. When we hear what he's claiming he was and claiming he did and claiming what happened to him…We worked right next to the man for a decade—I did, and other people for far longer than that and he was never any of those things. He was a miserable human being whose biggest accomplishment in his own eyes was how miserable could he make the people around him. Especially the people who were doing the most work. Those were the ones he really went after.

LIANA WIELAND, MIKE'S FORMER COLLEAGUE

He was rather snide and sarcastic toward staff, and I also noticed that his communications to staff were really demeaning. And if you have that kind of a tone being sort of spread through the organization, then that's kind of what happens—it changes the whole morale of the crew.

At the time, his deputy—clearly, in my viewpoint—did all the work. And Mike—it was pretty clear that he wasn't doing the work required and doing the work that he should be doing, and instead his deputy was solving the problems and getting a lot of the work done. Again, that goes back to his laziness.

One of the other things I observed was, I would have to go to his office every night to route him communication and he was always sleeping at his desk. I just don't know how he got much done. And it clearly wasn't him getting the work done around here, because he was either not around, sleeping, or didn't want to be associated with the crew. That's really what I observed.

KEN LONG, MIKE'S FORMER COLLEAGUE

Mike, rather than telling you exactly what was wrong or working with you, you got chopped up. He was not somebody that you wanted to trust.

I remember a practical joke he played on another one of our staff members that caused them to think they had caused some sort of terrible problem. And they were all in tears and crying and everybody had to then come in and calm them down. So, there was an aspect there of upsetting people.

There was also always a caution there of this is somebody you have to kind of keep your eyes open for to make sure that something isn't going to happen, whether it be physical or some sort of verbal attack or whatever. Because there were other times when I can recall being called up into his office a few times on one situation or another and he wouldn't be happy with the way I was handling it, would ask questions about it and the next thing I know would be chewing me out. But it wouldn't be "Ok, here's what you did wrong, here's what you should be doing." It was more like, "You're a stupid idiot, why the heck are you doing—why haven't you handled this."

SHEILA MACDONALD, MIKE'S FORMER COLLEAGUE

Mike Rinder was the least caring person I ever met. As a matter of fact, Mike Rinder is the one person that I met that is an example of someone that you would... the last person on Earth you would want to talk to is Mike Rinder, if you want to be a whole person yourself and sure of yourself.

I would describe him as a cold, calculating, conniving and totally false type of a person.

He would inevitably, for every single person, castigate them. He would invalidate them. He would say things about them that made them feel stupid and horrible. It was unbelievable. I couldn't believe this was happening.

He was constantly telling me how stupid I was, how minuscule, how I was a little low-level something or other. Not once did I ever get a comment from him that made me feel I could do my job.

He didn't ever get on with other people. He didn't ever apply, in my view and by my experience, Scientology technology—the technology of how to communicate with someone, how to develop good personal relationships. He had no good personal relationships. He made people terrified of him or made them so small that they didn't ever dare challenge him. It was how he got away with being such a sham. But anybody who uses him as a consultant is a fool.

ELAINE SIEGEL, MIKE'S FORMER COLLEAGUE

I remember one time Mike Rinder came over to Richard Wieland. We were sitting there at a table working on ads. And Mike Rinder walked over to Richard Wieland, and he had a pencil in his hand, and he says, "You do this one more time and I am going to stab you in the eyeball'. And he had it right close to Richard's eye like this. And it was just completely unbelievable, the violence—the intention was so violent—I have never seen any staff member do something like that.

RYAN PRESCOTT

LISA MCPHERSON
MEDICAL RECORD

AFFIDAVIT OF AMENDMENT TO MEDICAL CERTIFICATION OF DEATH
FLORIDA

SEE INSTRUCTIONS REVERSE SIDE					
...NDED INFORMATION CONCERNING DECEASED PERSON	1. NAME OF DECEASED (TYPE OR PRINT)	FIRST Lisa	MIDDLE	LAST McPherson	STATE FILE NO.
	2. DATE OF DEATH (Month, Day, Year) Dec 5, 1995	3a. PLACE OF DEATH (Check only one) HOSPITAL __ Inpatient X ER/Outpatient __ DOA OTHER: __ Nursing Home __ Residence __ Other (Specify)			3b. INSIDE CITY LIMITS? (Yes or No) Yes
	3c. FACILITY NAME (If not institution, give street and number) Columbia HCA New Port Richey Hospital		3d. CITY, TOWN, OR LOCATION OF DEATH New Port Richey		3e. COUNTY OF DEATH Pasco

AMENDED MEDICAL CERTIFICATION

		Approximate Interv Between Onset and Death
26. PART I. Enter the diseases, injuries, or complications that caused the death. Do not enter mode of dying, such as cardiac or respiratory arrest, shock, or heart failure. List only one cause on each line.		
IMMEDIATE CAUSE (Final disease or condition resulting in death) →	a. Pulmonary Thromboembolus	
	DUE TO (OR AS A CONSEQUENCE OF):	
Sequentially list conditions, if any, leading to immediate cause. Enter UNDERLYING CAUSE (Disease or injury that initiated events resulting in death) LAST.	b. Thrombotic Occlusion of Left Popliteal Vein with	
	DUE TO (OR AS A CONSEQUENCE OF):	
	c. Traumatic Hemorrhage of Left Popliteal Area	
	DUE TO (OR AS A CONSEQUENCE OF):	
	d.	

PART II. Other significant conditions contributing to death but not resulting in the underlying cause given in Part I	27a. WAS AN AUTOPSY PERFORMED? (Yes or No)	27b. WERE AUTOPSY FINDINGS AVAILABLE PRIOR TO COMPLETION OF CAUSE OF DEATH? (Yes or No)	28. CASE REPORTE TO MEDICAL EXAMINER? (Yes or No)
29. Psychosis & history of auto accident	Yes	Yes	Yes

29. IF FEMALE, WAS THERE A PREGNANCY IN THE PAST THREE MONTHS? □ Yes ☒ No	30a. IF SURGERY IS MENTIONED IN PART I OR II, ENTER CONDITION FOR WHICH IT WAS PERFORMED.		30b. DATE OF SURGERY (Mo., Day, Year)
31. PROBABLE MANNER OF DEATH (Specify: Accident, suicide, or homicide; or undetermined) Accident	32a. DATE OF INJURY (Mo., Day, Year) Unknown	32b. TIME OF INJURY Unkn M	32c. INJURY AT WORK? (Yes or No) No	32d. DESCRIBE HOW INJURY OCCURRED Received lower extremity trauma, exact etiology unknown
	32e. PLACE OF INJURY - At home, farm, street, factory, etc. (Specify) Unknown		32f. LOCATION (Street and Number or Rural Route Number, City or Town, State) Unknown

22a. To the best of my knowledge, death occurred at the time, date and place and due to the cause(s) as stated. (Signature and Title)	23a. On the basis of examination and/or investigation, in my opinion death occurred at the time, date and place and due to the cause(s) and manner as stat (Signature and Title)
22b. DATE SIGNED (Mo., Day, Year)	22c. HOUR OF DEATH M	23b. DATE SIGNED (Mo., Day, Year) Feb 16, 2000	23c. HOUR OF DEATH 9:51 P
22d. NAME OF ATTENDING PHYSICIAN IF OTHER THAN CERTIFIER (TYPE OR PRINT)	23d. MEDICAL EXAMINER'S CASE # 95.06.01474

24. NAME AND ADDRESS OF CERTIFIER (PHYSICIAN, MEDICAL EXAMINER) (Type or Print) Joan E. Wood, M.D., Dist. Med. Exam., 10850 Ulmerton Road, Largo, FL 33778

THE UNDERSIGNED, BEING FIRST DULY SWORN, STATES THAT THIS AFFIDAVIT IS MADE FOR THE PURPOSE OF AMENDING MEDICAL CERTIFICATION F THE ABOVE NAMED PERSON, AND THAT THE FOLLOWING EXPLANATION IS GIVEN AS THE BASIS OF THIS AMENDMENT:

Review of all case materials and consultation with other experts.

AFFIDAVIT	

SIGNATURE	(DEGREE OR TITLE) medical examiner	ADDRESS 10850 Ulmerton Road Largo, FL 33778	DATE SIGNED Feb 16, 2000
NOTARY	SUBSCRIBED AND SWORN TO BEFORE ME ON Feb. 16, 2000	SIGNATURE OF NOTARY Carol L. Zerwas	NOTARY OR NOTARY EXPIRES, DATE/SEAL CAROL R. ZERWAS Notary Public - State of Florida My Commission Expires Jan 24, 2003 Commission # CC804368
DH 434, 9/97	STATE REGISTRAR	BY	DATE FILED BY VITAL STATISTICS

MIKE RINDER STRIKED FROM L.A. SUPERIOR COURT

SUPERIOR COURT OF CALIFORNIA, COUNTY OF LOS ANGELES
Civil Division
Central District, Stanley Mosk Courthouse, Department 57

December 30, 2020

Objecting Defendants CSI and CCI also point the Court to a March 6, 2020 declaration by Michael Rinder, which was submitted in support of Plaintiffs' prior opposition to a motion compel arbitration that was taken off calendar (due to the filing of the first amended complaint).

Defendants argue the Court should disregard the March 6, 2020 declaration because Rinder is biased, dedicated to falsely attacking the Church and has no foundation for much of his testimony. CSI and CCI also make specific objections to the declaration.

Plaintiffs were given leave to properly submit the declaration in support of the oppositions to the instant motions. Plaintiffs submitted the same declaration that was submitted on March 6, 2020. Upon review of the declaration Defendants objections to the declaration are sustained. The declaration is filled with unsupported assumptions, foundational deficiencies, irrelevant matters, improper opinions, and arguments.

MARK RATHBUN ON CLEARWATER STUNT

He says in the thing that he—he says in this story that he, Mike Rinder says that he moved to Clearwater so that he would be visible to his son Benjamin who was working in Clearwater. I was there. Never came up. He moved to Clearwater because I got him a free ride gig with a guy that would pay him to do nothing but talk out about Scientology. Nothing to do with Benjamin, his son.

Okay. To highlight the point, I don't know, a few months after he was there, Rinder took great offense to the fact that the Church was responding to him attacking the Church by saying, "Well, he left his kids behind and doesn't care about them," right. And he would bemoan that over and over and over again, right. And so, I said, "Hey, if it bothers you that much that people are saying that, why don't we go down and attempt to go see your kid. The Church isn't going to let us, and therefore we can put it on tape, and it can show that you did have concern for your kid, but they didn't allow it to happen." Oh, Rinder was all happy about that. "That sounds great."

It had nothing to do with seeing his kid, alright. Because he knew it was going to be rejected. It had to do with his own personal reputation and him responding to accusations that were made about him in public. And when we went to the Fort Harrison, the Church's headquarters in Clearwater, as predicted, they said, "You can't come here," and they gave us a trespassing warning. "You've got to leave. And in fact, we called the police." So, I said, "Hang on. Let's wait and see the police. So, the police showed up, and the police said, "We're giving you a trespass warning. You got to leave." I explained to them why we were there—that Mike wanted to see his son, who worked there. And the cop said, "Hey, I can go in there and see him. And in the presence of nobody, tell him that you're here to see him. And if he wants to come, we'll escort him right out to see you, if it's, you're worried, as you say, that the Church isn't allowing it to happen."

Rinder's like, "No, no, that's okay." I said, "No, no, let's do it." He didn't want to do it. I said, "Let's do it." So it put him in a bad position and the cop said, "Okay." And the cop went in there—20-30 minutes later came back. And he said, "I got to talk to him alone and Benjamin doesn't want to see you. And he's an adult. And it's his red, white, and blue American-born right to exercise that prerogative."

You know, Rinder has stated that he was the great warrior for Scientology, right—without ever disclosing anything he ever did that was nefarious. Just saying that he did—that he silenced people, and he was the hit man. But nobody ever got hit, and there was no silencing that we've heard of. And so, she, [Leah] Remini exonerates him of all this and says, "You're fighting now against the Church so you're on the right side of the fight now." End of quote, right. And this is what I'm talking about. He's absolved by the fact that he's on board with this cult.

ON-SCREEN TITLE: ASC (Anti-Scientology Cult)

This cult that says that they're the enemy and anything you do in furtherance of weakening the enemy is A-Okay.

And so, the thing—the crux of the story that keeps on being replayed with Rinder is, this great justification that he must continue to crusade against Scientology, because of his two children that are in Scientology, okay. And they omit the fact that he left with Scientology—he left Scientology without ever reaching out to or making any kind of gesture whatsoever to any of his family, to try to get somebody to go with him, or to explain himself, or to be talked back or to any of that. He just, he just took off, right. Number one.

Number two, he just denigrates his kids. I mean, I have reality on one of them in particular because I know his daughter Taryn. I probably worked more closely with her than he ever did, based on my position in the Church, because she was in the technical, Qualifications division. And so, I had a lot of back and forth. And I mean—and I've had this conversation with Rinder. I mean, he knows. I've made this known to him and he hasn't disagreed. His continuing to crusade, his continuing to denigrate Scientology, his continuing to belittle Scientology, okay, is the worst possible thing he could ever do in terms of ever reconciling with his son and daughter. And yet he continues to do it.

I mean, it goes to new extremes in this series with Remini, to the point where he literally makes statements that are denigrating to Taryn and Benjamin, personally, saying, "There couldn't possibly be any reason"— "There couldn't possibly be any input in the decision for them to not be in communication with me." In other words, they are just mindless automatons who are taking orders from the Church.

First of all, he doesn't—he has no basis to know that, because he chose to leave, what, eight years earlier, now? By the way, you know, the time just gets screwed around with—we don't realize, all this happened eight years ago, right—nine years ago. Ten years ago. It's ten years ago now. I mean, that's how long ago this is. And they make it sound like it's all—this is all new, fresh stuff. He left ten years ago, with a "good riddance," essentially, to them, Benjamin, and Taryn.

And—so what it amounts to, literally, is he's, Mike Rinder is literally being paid by Leah Remini to go up there and denigrate and call his kids a bunch of mindless automatons and then have the temerity to say, "Hey, this is all I can do, I'm doing this for my children." It's really sick, it's really twisted.

MARK RATHBUN ON SETTING UP RINDER'S GIGS

God, it's been ten years since he left, and he literally for an entire decade has not worked, and I arranged virtually all of his gigs with people that would pay him to just do anti-Scientology stuff.

First there was this guy down in Clearwater. He lasted about, I don't know, only a few weeks and the guy just couldn't tolerate Rinder being around, so he got fired. Then it was this guy Almblad, who was an alcoholic, who just would go into these alcohol-fueled rants and rages about bringing David Miscavige to his knees and destroying Miscavige. And he just had this complete obsession, and Rinder would just pump that up, and tell him how possible all this stuff was and how they could attack the trademarks and rip off the copyrights, and all this other kind of stuff.

And, you know, my conversations with the guy were, you know, kind of talking him off the ledge about how that's kind of a neat pipe dream but the practicalities are, it ain't going to happen. You're in no legal position to do it. And he could—and he didn't like that, but he continued to "employ" Rinder for another two years, to have him stroke him with those fantasies, had him living in his—rent-free in a home and the whole thing.

Then there was this other guy, Michael Bennitt, who came along, who said—called himself a venture capitalist from Chicago. He came all the way to south Texas to see me, and was, you know, he—first of all, first, he just walked up to me in a coffee shop in San Antonio. Rinder was there, acting like this little groupie about, you know, "I really admire you," and this, that, and the other thing. He was trying to sleaze in on me, and I said, "God, this guy's really creepy." And Mike of course, being Mickey the Dunce, Mickey the, you know, ingratiator, said, "Oh yeah, I agree, Marty." Right?

Then that Bennitt guy, two months later, comes all the way down to south Texas to my home in Corpus Christi, and he's running the same thing on wanting to, you know, be my benefactor, be my partner, or some kind of thing. And I'm like, I couldn't get him out of my house fast enough, he was that creepy.

Well, I didn't actually arrange that gig—I guess I did indirectly by rejecting the guy, because three months later, or several months later, all of a sudden Rinder tells me he's working for this Michael Bennitt guy. The long and the short of that, I said, "What are you doing?" He says, "I'm doing public relations." I said, "Okay. What are you—what have you actually done?" He said, "Well, the only thing I did, I"—you know, he had this woman who was sort of eccentric, who had tons of money; she got a huge divorce settlement, and she had nothing better to do so she created a gelato company. "Doesn't know the first thing about it, but—so I was doing PR." "Like what?" He said, "Well, basically, I did TRs—training routines, Scientology training routines—to teach her how to feel comfortable communicating." And that's all he did.

And then there's Karen de la Carriere, who, you know, I've described before, and she wants to be the center of the universe. And I don't know how she makes her money, but she makes a lot of it and she passes it out.

But she wants lots of face time and lots of influence and I, you know, I finally told her, "Just don't even send me any money," because she'd become so meddling. I said, "I'm not going to be influenced by your—you know, I told you that from the beginning, and you just won't learn; I'm not going to do it." Well, of course, Mike doesn't have those rules. He'll do or say whatever anybody wants him to, as long as there's grease, right. And so, she's been greasing him the whole time, and she famously makes it known to others that he cannot turn on her or say anything negative about her, pursuant to ASC [Anti-Scientology Cult] "rules," because she's his matron.

And so, you know, the Aftermath—that's the, that's the "Premath," okay? The Aftermath is him playing with his latest benefactor, Leah Remini, because I know for a fact: She told me I could write my own ticket to take that place and I rejected the gig—just like I did with the other ones, who want to tell me what I'm going to say and do.

MARK RATHBUN ON MONEY INFLUENCES RINDER

That's the Mike Rinder I know. He gloms onto people. He's like a mirror. He's like he doesn't exist as an independent entity. He gloms on and feeds back to you and just gives you positive feedback.

He's the classic passive-aggressive, like you can go look up passive-aggressive in Wikipedia or Psychology Today or anywhere else and look at the definition—the guy fits it to a T.

He—you know, it states right in there—speaks very diplomatically, appears very cooperative, right, but all the while is busily, quietly, and passively stabbing you in the back, okay. And that's Mike Rinder, right. And he gets a—he's a professional to go along to get along or get along to go along, right, and so that's what he does. He did it in the Church, he did it with me, he did it with all the five sugar daddies he got that have financed him since he got out of the Church, and he's doing it with Leah Remini.

So, no matter what she says—and that's what this whole series [Scientology and the Aftermath] is degenerating into—he's saying less and less, she's saying more and more, yet he's the consultant, you know, insider who's supposed to have all the firsthand data. She's saying more and more and he's just saying, "Uh-huh, yeah." He's like the bobbing-head doll. "Uh-huh, Leah. Yeah. Uh-huh. Yeah. Right, I hundred percent agree with you." Right—because that's what Mike Rinder does. Okay, and so my point is, is that, you know, even if this is affected, all of these positive things he's saying about Scientology, many years after he's left, right, the one fact remains: he is an inveterate liar.

The truth aligns depending upon from where his bread is being buttered. Okay. The sugar daddies were paying for access to me through Mike, right. And they were paying for axes that they wanted to grind with Scientology. So, you could just analyze all of his statements from 2009— 2007 when he left Scientology to the present (he's been out for 10 years, almost 11) and you will see, I could show you the financial interests that led to, to the truth he was espousing at the time. And that is most blatantly true on the Leah Remini show where this guy's making ungodly sums of money by simply being her Winchell Mahoney, you know, being her ventriloquist dummy that validates and gives her positive feedback on the stuff she invents.

MARK RATHBUN ON RINDER'S LITIGATION TACTIC

So, Mike Rinder has been the chief capper for anti-Scientology lawyers, the guy who goes out—the ambulance chaser—who goes out and finds somebody and dresses up something and brings it back to a PI [Personal Injury] lawyer and gets his thing. And it's a great gig.

Of course, he's laughing all the way to the bank because he's making 175 bucks an hour for being a capper ambulance chaser who goes and finds—drums people up to bring litigation, encourages them, brings them to PI lawyers, okay.

And the only reason I mention that is that, you know, the people that he has suckered into bringing lawsuits have wound up having their heads handed to them and created precedents protecting Scientology and destroying the "rights to recover" that he was promoting as something they were deserving of, right?

And he's laughing all the way to the bank and the ASC [Anti-Scientology Cult] doesn't know—because they—you know, how well compensated he is in this whole litigation scam because Backpage [Backpage.com] Tony [Ortega] reports on the hearing where Rinder's cross-examined on his compensation, and Backpage Tony says, "And, believe me, it's not much." Right.

Months later the transcript somehow wound up with me, and what Backpage Tony failed to report was he [Rinder] gets $175 an hour for creating those results for these people.

Okay, and of course at the end of the last season making a big production about how he was going to this big white-shoe firm in New York to go take down Scientology, right. Right. And he went through that exercise and charade with me eight years earlier, right, and he's the guy here that's telling you—now he's telling you, now that he's got paid for all that, "Don't want to engage in this lightly."

MARK RATHBUN ON RINDER'S PART IN LEAH REMINI'S STAGED EXIT

Rinder explained to me that they had literally worked out—the three of them, the troika—had literally worked out an operation where Leah's departure from Scientology would be orchestrated, okay. And it would be reported in a way that they wanted to manipulate it being reported, which was completely and utterly an act. It was a classic troll job.

Leah would act as if she were being persecuted by Scientology for disagreeing with it and for having all this "scandalous" information about it. All the while, she was orchestrating and having her agents create the story of her leaving. And it was done in such a way as to try to create a reaction on the part of Scientology, to get Scientology—it was a sting operation to try to get Scientology to reach out to try to salvage her, to get Scientology to have people disconnect from her, all of which would be part of the ongoing story.

And it was all going to be a rollout to increase her profile and create this mystery and create this figure who was this warrior princess, innocent warrior princess. She'd be this innocent princess who was converted into a warrior because she was hunted down and persecuted by Scientology. Okay, that was the story. And they literally—and you know, as it rolled out, Scientology never played its part. And they just acted like it did. In other words, she never did get persecuted, she never did get hunted down, she never did get people begging her to come back. None of that stuff happened. But Rinder and Ortega just kept spinning the ball, giving the impression that it did.

You know, this op that is run by Rinder, Remini and Ortega is—and the reason why I refer to them as a troika and as a cluster at the top of this thing is that they have this penchant for having one arm of them, they act like Mickey the Dunce whenever one of them does something.

You know, that's how they rolled out Leah Remini in the first place. Tony Ortega literally reported as if he were onto a hot tip from a "tipster." The tipster was Leah Remini—you know, like an insider that knew what was going on with Leah. And he literally quoted Leah's husband. He reported that he called Leah's husband and said, "Hey, we heard you're having a big break with the Church of Scientology," and her husband reportedly said, "Oh no, no, not at all. We get along just peachy keen. And if we ever did we would resolve it with the Church." And Tony Ortega say—goes all the way as to saying, "And we thanked him for being so candid," right. Well, the whole thing was scripted by Leah Remini and her husband and Mike Rinder and Tony Ortega. So, it was like they literally made up this news. And that's how the whole thing ran down—rolled out and started.

And so, they continue that whole op to today, where one of them does something, the other one can say, "Well, that's not—I didn't, I don't know anything about that."

MARK RATHBUN EXPOSES "MISSING PERSON" SCAM

One of the critical parts of the Rinder-Ortega-Remini rollout of Remini was the "missing" Shelly Miscavige, the wife of [Scientology ecclesiastical leader] David Miscavige. And you know, at the time, in 2013, I think it was, Rinder told me about that—that she was going to do a whole thing about "Where's Shelly?" and going to put the Church in just an unbelievably terrible position because, you know, he figured it all out, because he's been in public relations his entire life.

And he figured it all out. There was going to be this untenable position where nobody could respond to it because it is so personal and it's so—the accusation is so—one of those things like a "Do you beat your wife?" conundrum, right, the way they're framing the accusation, that they could just go to town and make it into a, you know, a series, a serial that just keeps playing out, right.

And I said, "Mike, why would Leah do something like this, you know, if she has any concern about her own credibility and integrity? You know she's not missing. You know that Leah Remini truly doesn't have the rank to ask—to know exactly where she is, when, and how she does her business. That just as much as she feels like, you know, that she needs the ability to be wherever she wants and associate with whomever she wants, Shelly has the exact same right. The last—and you know that—the last person in the world she'd want to see is Leah Remini or Mike Rinder."

Mike goes, "Yeah, yeah, I know, I know. I know all that but it's like this perfect thing because it puts them in a position where this is the wife of the head of Scientology. It puts them in this untenable position." He knew. He knew it was a scam from the beginning. He knew it was a cheap shot from the beginning.

I was certain that Rinder conned her on the Shelly story being a story of manufacture, and then when I called her out on it she said, "Oh yeah, I already knew that. I was running a false black PR campaign the entire time."

I said, "You know, Mike Rinder knows this is a scam and a sham. And I could have—if you had asked me about it and asked my opinion you wouldn't have gotten into this in the first place." She goes, "I know that, I knew she wasn't missing." In other words, she told me she's in complete and utter league and agreement with Mike Rinder.

I thought at that point I was giving her the benefit of the doubt, maybe she's just being taken advantage of because Mike, because Mike, he'll do any—he'll say, you know, that's what he is famous for. He's the most agreeable guy on the planet and people, you know, find that reassuring to have him around them, so he's making good, regular bucks by playing that role for her. But no, she knew that. And that was cool with her. In other words, she knew it was a scam from the beginning.

The amazing thing is, here we are, okay, that was 2014, '15, '16— we're three years later and they're still running it. Every several months or so they roll the thing out again, they'll come out with an event, a PR event. She'll file an FOI [Freedom of Information] request with the police, right. And Ortega will run this big thing and he'll try to get it out to the tabloids.

She's complaining because the police aren't investigating the Shelly thing, right. They get their documents, their responses, no further story, right, because there's nothing there. But, you know, they don't inform the troll farm—so all these people are living in this alternate reality, that they believe this world view that they're being fed by Remini, Rinder and Ortega who are laughing all the way to the bank.

HANDWRITTEN LETTER
TO DAVID MISCAVIGE

Mike Rinder

21 August 2003

Re: My Honesty

Dear Sir (David Miscavige),

Thank you for coming by to see me and _____ tonight - and I want to apologize for wasting your time and creating further enterbulation. I sat down and really did some soul searching with the assistance of the others as I obviously still had not confronted the depths of my out ethics and suppressive acts.

Many times I've looked at the overts I've committed when I have lied to you, and I've always had the idea that it was bad because it had caused upset - but not really confronted it as a basic violation of integrity, and therefore something far more fundamental and degraded - it is a reflection of my cowardice and lack of integrity that I would do this and it's just black and white wrong and a low-toned suppressive trait. I've done it many times with you and have always had some justification for it that I then didn't really confront it for what it is. I finally confronted this for real - there's no justification or Q&A about it. It's wrong, it's low-toned, and especially under the circumstances of being in the midst of a war, it's suppressive. I don't mean it's OK at any time, it's not - but the times I have done this with you have been when my "neck" has been so precious to me that I have been willing to put you and the Church in danger because of it.

I looked at a lot of things that finally opened this door - because I felt I was still to some degree trying to hold onto some rightness - which is why I didn't answer "me" when you asked who was the worst last night, and the comm lag tonight.

I went back to the time in CMO CW and the "successful actions" from that time. I've always hung onto the idea that there were things right about that time, and the operating basis with (illegible) was to always "be a good subordinate" and always say things are under control - unless it was reporting on someone else being a screw-up. But never was I a screw-up or responsible for anything wrong other than "handling someone else". This is the thing I contronted - that whole scene was an out-ethics sham. I see now this false assertion is just that - a false assertion that I've held in place to prove I'm right.

This then led (lead) me to really confront my integrity with respect to telling the truth and how I hate myself about this no matter how I justify it.

I know I have taken a long time to have this realization - and you have pointed it out to me many times and I've never been willing to look at this for the black and white issue it is - because it's a point of my own integrity first, and violating my own integrity has caused terrible results.

I do appreciate your insistence that I actually confront this - it actually was a major realization and relief to see something that is so obvious to you and others. With all the justifications I have had in place, telling the truth under certain circumstances was in my universe no different than telling a lie or withholding - but that is no longer the case, as I've finally recovered my integrity on this and will never operate in this suppressive fashion again.

This is OK,

ML (Much Love),
Mike (Rinder)

COST OF AN ANTI-CULT AFFIDAVIT

Professor Stephen Kent, a professor at the University of Alberta, has emerged in recent years, as a traveling crusader against academic scholars of new religious movements who threaten the profession's integrity by, inter alia, appearing as expert witnesses on behalf of religious movements.

Kent has recently appeared in Germany and Denmark to promote his crusade.

Anti-Scientologists have now posted on the Web his affidavit against the Church of Scientology in the well-known McPherson civil case. As far as I know, Kent has not objected to the posting, nor has he suggested that the document has not been faithfully reproduced. It is a document of 12,825 words (bibliography included). Of particular interest is the last paragraph:

"My curriculum vitae is attached to this report, and it lists all of my publications for the past ten years along with court cases in which I testified as an expert. For preparing this report I have been compensated at the rate of $200.00 per hour. I have worked approximately 55 hours on it. The exhibits that I plan to use in support of my opinion are included in my bibliography."

Thus, the cost of the affidavit comes to $11,000. Readers familiar with Kent's private and public production will easily recognize that most of the affidavit is derived from Kent's previous works. At any rate, if Kent really thinks that experts in "cult" cases should make $11,000 for each 13.000-words document based on their previous works they write, he may be right after all and "academic integrity" may, in fact, be in serious danger.

Massimo Introvigne, Feb. 18, 2000

ANTI-CULT AFFIDAVIT
$21,600

I have commented before on Prof. Stephen Kent's crusade to preserve integrity in the study of new religious movements against monetary corruptions, and the (corresponding?) increasingly high costs of his affidavits. He has of course argued that scholars executing affidavits on behalf of new religious movements also receive significant amounts of money. Obviously, this is not the point. These scholars do not tour the world to lecture against money-induced corruption of scholarly studies about new religious movements. Kent does, and it is not unfair to suggest that he should be judged by his own standards.

For those who have heard Kent downplay the religious element in Scientology, a recommended reading is now Kent's affidavit in the Texas case EEOC v. I-20 Animal Medical Center, signed on November 9, 1999. In the case, EEOC charged that the use of Scientology-based training methods in the workplace violates Title VII since Scientology is a religion and not a purely secular training system. Supporting EEOC, Kent signed an affidavit to the effect that this is a case of "intrusion of religious concepts into the workplace" (p. 9). The courses contained "Scientology terms" that Kent now describes as being "purely religious".

In short, the courses "contained the Scientology religion" (pp. 12-13). Quite correctly, Kent concludes that Scientology is a religion based mostly on its notions of thetan and of past lives. We applaud Kent's reliance (at least) on mainline scholarship on Scientology in order to come to the conclusion that what others (including persons Kent should know better than any other) have described as mere "treatment" is in fact "a religious practice" (p. 18). If somebody should accuse him of incoherence, Kent would of course answer that he always claimed that Scientology is also, but not exclusively a religion, a fine distinction probably lost to the audiences and courts that received Kent's previous wisdom. For the 19-pages affidavit, Kent "has been compensated at the rate of $ 200.00 per hour" and has "worked approximately 108 hours to date". That raises the cost of a Kent affidavit (although, admittedly, not a typical one) to $21,600.

Massimo Introvigne

L. RON HUBBARD ABOUT CANCELED POLICY

I, L. Ron Hubbard, being duly sworn, depose and say that:

1. I am the founder of the Religion of the Church of Scientology.

2. From time to time, over the past 20 years I have written doctrine known as "Policy Letters" which are currently in use as administered by the Churches' ministerial staff.

3. On and around March 17, 1965; March 7, 1965 and December 23, 1965; I had cause to write three "Policy letters" entitled "Suppressive Acts Suppression of Scientology and Scientologists The Fair Game Law" (7 March 1965 and 23 December 1965) and "Fair Game Law Organization Suppressive Acts The Source of the Fair Game Law" (17 March 1965).

4. These policies were written with the intent to remove some of the fundamental barriers from the progress of the Church and its parishioners.

5. The intent, as written by me, was simply to make it clear to all Scientologists that those who actively attempted to block our forward progress could no longer be considered a member of the group and thusly not be afforded the protection of Scientology Ethics as so covered in the volumes of policy on the subject of ethics as written by myself.

Scientologists in good standing are protected by the ethical policies of the Church against suits or disturbances of any kind by another Scientologist. Recourse from any such action is immediately available to any Scientologist via a Chaplain's court which is held by a Scientology minister. His function is to settle all differences amicably.

6. There was never any attempt or intent on my part by the writing of these policies (or any others for that fact), to authorize illegal or

harassment type acts against anyone.

7. As soon as it became apparent to me that the concept of "Fair Game" as described above was being misinterpreted by the uninformed, to mean the granting of a license to Scientologists for acts in violation of the law and/or other standards of decency, these policies were cancelled.

The handling of a Suppressive person with regards to the fact that he is not accepted within the Church and may not avail himself of Chaplain's Courts and other services of the Church due to the fact that he causes trouble and does not make personal gains, remains a stringent Church policy.

Signed this __22nd_ day of ___March__ 1976.

(signed)
L. Ron Hubbard

RYAN PRESCOTT

GLOSSARY

A&E Network: an American television network, the flagship television property of A&E Networks. It is headquartered in New York City. (Wikipedia)

Aberration: a departure from rational thought or behavior.

Advanced Organization (AO): ministers advanced services, providing training through Class VIII and auditing through New OT V.

At an Advanced Organization, the individual recovers lost abilities and gains new insights into the nature of his own spirituality, his relationship to others, the material universe, and the Eighth Dynamic. Thus, it is not surprising to find that an atmosphere of spiritual discovery permeates these Churches. Those who come to an Advanced Organization have studied diligently to reach this point on the Bridge and ascending the OT levels is a significant step. It is here that individuals fully recover true certainty of their own spirituality and become confident of their ability to play and win the game of life—not only today but far into the future.

Affidavit: a written statement confirmed by oath or affirmation, for use as evidence in court. (Oxford)

Allegation: (n) A claim or assertion that someone has done something illegal or wrong, typically one made without proof. (Oxford)

Alley, Kirstie: Scientologist. Kirstie Louise Alley is an American actress and spokesmodel. She first achieved recognition in 1982, playing Saavik in the science fiction film *Star Trek II: The Wrath of Khan*. Alley played Rebecca Howe on the NBC sitcom *Cheers*, receiving an Emmy Award and a Golden Globe in 1991 for the role. (Wikipedia)

Allure: (v) Powerfully attract or charm; tempt.

Alter: (v) Change in character or composition, typically in a comparatively small but significant way. (Oxford)

American Saint Hill Organization (ASHO): home to the Saint Hill Special Briefing Course and the legendary Power Processes. The Ideal ASHO is entirely transformed to accommodate unprecedented numbers moving up the Bridge with speed in this Golden Age of Tech Phase II. Located on L. Ron Hubbard Way in Los Angeles, California.

Analytical Mind: the conscious aware **mind** which thinks, observes data, remembers it, and resolves problems. It would be essentially the conscious **mind** as opposed to the unconscious mind. In Dianetics and Scientology the **analytical mind** is the one which is alert and aware and the reactive mind simply reacts without **analysis.**

Anti-Scientology Cult (ASC): A small and corrupt group of individuals united for the purpose of attacking Scientology. Their mission is to attack the Church of Scientology for publicity and money. These individuals are to project what they're doing onto the Church of Scientology and Scientologists.

Antisocial Personality: there are certain characteristics and mental attitudes which cause about 20 percent of a race to violently oppose any betterment activity or group.

Apostate: (n) a person who abandons his or her religion, party, cause, etc. (Collins English Dictionary)

Applied Scholastics: a nonprofit, public benefit corporation dedicated to improving education with L. Ron Hubbard's learning and literacy tools, collectively known as Study Technology.

Aptitude Test: (n) a test designed to determine a person's ability in a particular skill or field of knowledge. (Oxford)

Artifact: (n) An object made by a human being, typically an item of cultural or historical interest. (Oxford)

Auditing (Pastoral Counseling): from the Latin audire meaning "to hear or listen", is the name given to a range of Scientology procedures intended to help people become aware of their spiritual nature and more able in life. Auditing can be ministered to a group (such as at a Scientology Sunday service) or to an individual on a one-to-one basis. A person can also minister certain auditing to himself. All Scientology churches have rooms designated for auditing. (Church of Scientology International)

Auditor: defined as one who listens, from the Latin audire meaning to hear or listen. An auditor is a minister or minister-in-training of the Church of Scientology. (Church of Scientology International)

Backpage: was a classified advertising website that had become the largest marketplace for buying and selling sex by the time that federal law enforcement agencies seized it in April 2018.

Blackmail: (n) The action, treated as a criminal offense, of demanding

Degrade: (v) Lower the character or quality of.

Deposition: (n) A formal, usually written, statement to be used as evidence. (Oxford)

Deprogram: (v) Release (someone) from apparent brainwashing, typically that of a religious cult, by the systematic re-indoctrination of conventional values. (Oxford)

Despicable: (adj.) Deserving hatred and contempt.

Dianetics: The word Dianetics is derived from the Greek dia, meaning "through," and nous, "mind or soul." Dianetics is further defined as "what the soul is doing to the body." When the mind adversely affects the body, it is described as a psychosomatic condition. Psycho refers to "mind or soul" and somatic refers to "body." Thus, psychosomatic illnesses are physical illnesses caused by the soul.

L. Ron Hubbard discovered the single source of nightmares, unreasonable fears, upsets, insecurities, and psychosomatic illness—the reactive mind. In his book Dianetics: The Modern Science of Mental Health he described the reactive mind in detail and laid out a simple, practical, easily taught technology to overcome it and reach the state of Clear. Dianetics is that technology.

Disgruntled: (adj.) Angry or dissatisfied (Oxford)

Distilled: (adj.) Having been shortened so that only the essential meaning or most important aspects remain.

E-Meter: E-Meter is a shortened term for electropsychometer. It is a religious artifact used as a spiritual guide in auditing. It is for use only by a Scientology minister or a Scientology minister-in-training to help the preclear locate and confront areas of spiritual upset.

Ecclesiastical: (adj.) of or relating to a church, especially as an established institution (Merriam-Webster)

Epitomize: (v) Be a perfect example of.

Enterbulation: agitation or disturbance; commotion and upset.

Entheta: a compound word meaning enterbulated theta, theta in a turbulent state, agitated or disturbed. (Theta is the energy of thought and life. Theta is reason, serenity, stability, happiness, cheerful emotion, persistence, and the other factors which Man ordinarily considers desirable. The complete description of theta is contained in *Science of Survival* by L. Ron Hubbard.)

Ethics Officer(s): the person in a Scientology organization who has the following purpose: To help Ron clear organizations and the public if need be, of entheta and enterbulation so that Scientology can be done.

Expose: (v) Make (something) visible by uncovering it. (Oxford)

Exteriorization: the state of the thetan, the individual himself, being outside the body with or without full perception, but still able to control and handle the body.

Fair Game: A policy written by L. Ron Hubbard and canceled in 1968 based on misconceptions, misinterpretations, and misapplications. This policy meant that any Scientologists being attacked by a Suppressive Person may take this outside of the Scientology Ethics System and directly to a Court of Law. This is used today, incorrectly, by the Anti-Scientology Cult members to attack the Church in litigation with lawyers like Gerry Armstrong and Ken Dandar. This policy has been rewritten by the Anti-Scientologists and is being used by those wanting to ruthlessly attack Scientology.

Fall prey to (also be or become prey to): Be vulnerable to or overcome by. (Oxford)

Field Staff Members (FSM): individual Scientologists who disseminate Scientology and help raise funds for the Church by providing basic Scientology books to interested friends, family members and acquaintances, and introducing other interested individuals to the Church. Field staff members are appointed by their nearest Scientology Church. Because they have had immense spiritual gains from Dianetics and Scientology, field staff members naturally want to share the technology with others.

Flabbergast: (v) Surprise (someone) greatly; astonish. (Oxford)

Flag Service Organization (Flag): a religious retreat located in Clearwater, Florida. It serves as the spiritual headquarters for Scientologists planet wide. Flag is the largest Church of Scientology in the world. Flag represents the hub of the greater Scientology worldwide community as a dynamic, multilingual organization. Flag not only ministers the most advanced levels of training available anywhere, but all advanced levels of auditing up to New OT VII.

The title "Flag" follows from the fact that from the late 1960s through the mid-1970s, the highest ecclesiastical organizations were located at sea aboard a flotilla of ships. The 330-foot motor vessel Apollo served as Mr. Hubbard's home. Accordingly, it was then the most senior Scientology Church. It was known as the "Flagship" of the flotilla and called "Flag" for short.

Foundation for a Drug-Free World: a nonprofit organization headquartered in Los Angeles, California, and dedicated to the eradication of illicit drugs, their abuse, and their attendant criminality.

Freewinds: a 440-foot ship based in the Caribbean. Its home port is Curacao. The ship, in turn, is the home of the Flag Ship Service Organization (FSSO), a religious retreat ministering the most advanced level of spiritual counseling in the Scientology religion.

The Freewinds provides a safe, aesthetic, distraction-free environment appropriate for ministration of this profoundly spiritual level of auditing. Thus, while the Flag Service Organization in Clearwater ministers the highest levels of training and auditing from the bottom of the Bridge to New OT VII, the most advanced OT level (New OT VIII) is exclusively entrusted to the FSSO.

Golden Era Productions: the center for all audiovisual productions for the Scientology religion, responsible for producing, translating, and making all of L. Ron Hubbard's films, recorded lectures and printed scripture known and available to 11,000 Churches, missions and affiliated groups in 165 countries.

Hubbard Guidance Center (HGC): the Department of Processing in a Church of Scientology organization where auditing is delivered to preclears.

Ideal: (adj.) Satisfying one's conception of what is perfect; most suitable. (Oxford)

Immunity: (n) Protection or exemption from something, especially an obligation or penalty. (Oxford)

Impression: (n) An idea, feeling, or opinion about something or someone, especially one formed without conscious thought or on the basis of little evidence. (Oxford)

Inaugurate: (v) Mark the beginning or first public use of (an organization or project) with a special event or ceremony. (Oxford)

Inextricably: (adverb) In a way that is impossible to disentangle or separate. (Oxford)

Infiltrate: (v) Enter or gain access to (an organization, place, etc.) surreptitiously and gradually, especially in order to acquire secret information. (Oxford)

Innuendo: (n) An allusive or oblique remark or hint, typically a suggestive or disparaging one. (Oxford)

Internal Revenue Service (IRS): a U.S. government agency responsible for the collection of taxes and enforcement of tax laws.

International Association of Scientologists (IAS): an unincorporated membership organization open to all Scientologists from all nations.

International Hubbard Ecclesiastical League of Pastors (I HELP):

created to aid auditors who minister religious services in the field and thus outside organized Churches.

International Justice Chief (IJC): the executive in Senior HCO International responsible for the standard application of Scientology Justice policies to staff and public. He is a protector of the Church and its tenets and membership. His duties include reviewing and approving (or not approving) any major justice actions to ensure that no injustice is done. He is assisted by Continental Justice Chiefs in each Continental Senior HCO.

Introspection Rundown: an auditing rundown which helps a preclear locate and correct those things which cause him to have his attention inwardly fixated. He then becomes capable of looking outward so he can see his environment, handle, and control it.

L. Ron Hubbard: L. Ron Hubbard was an author, philosopher, humanitarian, and Founder of the Scientology religion. He was born March 13, 1911, in Tilden, Nebraska, and passed away January 24, 1986.

Liberation: (n) Freedom from limits on thought or behavior. (Oxford)

Lobotomy: (n) A surgical operation involving incision into the prefrontal lobe of the brain, formerly used to treat mental illness. (Oxford)

LRH: Initials of L. Ron Hubbard, Founder of Scientology and Dianetics

Masterson, Danny: Scientologist. Daniel Peter Masterson is an American actor and disc jockey. Masterson played the roles of Steven Hyde in *That '70s Show* and Jameson "Rooster" Bennett in *The Ranch*. (Wikipedia)

Minton, Robert: Investor. Sponsored witch hunts against Scientology in Clearwater, FL, one Anti-Scientology film, interviewed on multiple talk shows, and lost over $7,000,000 after being conned by members of the Anti-Scientology Cult. One of the investors of the Lisa McPherson Trust and exposed it from the inside with two scathing affidavits against Anti-Scientologists and corrupt lawyer, Ken Dandar.

Miscavige, David: the ecclesiastical leader of the Scientology religion. From his position as Chairman of the Board of Religious Technology Center (RTC), Mr. Miscavige bears the ultimate responsibility for ensuring the standard and pure application of L. Ron Hubbard's technologies of Dianetics and Scientology and for Keeping Scientology Working. (Scientology)

Moderator: (n) An arbitrator or mediator. (Oxford)

Motivator(s): acts received by the person or individual causing injury, reduction, or degradation of his beingness, person, associations, or dynamics. A motivator is called a "motivator" because it tends to prompt an overt. When a person commits an overt or overt of omission with no motivator, he tends to believe or pretends that he has received a motivator which does not in fact exist. This is a false motivator. Beings suffering from this are said to have "motivator hunger" and are often aggrieved over nothing.

Narconon: a highly effective drug-free withdrawal, detoxification and rehabilitation program which utilizes techniques developed by L. Ron Hubbard. Narconon, meaning "no drugs," began as a grass-roots movement in the mid-1960s when an inmate of the Arizona State Prison solved his own drug problem using principles found in one of L. Ron Hubbard's books. He then used those same principles to help solve drug-related problems of fellow inmates.

Narrative: (n) A spoken or written account of connected events; a story.

Non-Profit: (adj.) Not making or conducted primarily to make a profit. (Oxford)

Of (or by or on) one's own volition: (n) Voluntarily.

Ortega, Tony: Anti-Religious Blogger. Once hired by the Village Voice, wrote over 100 conspiracy theories against the Church of Scientology, fired due to his connection with Backpage (the prostitution sex ring online) and Village Voice's ties, he was paid off. Anti-Scientology Cult member and Propagandist.

Operating Thetan (OT): a spiritual state of being above Clear. By Operating is meant "able to act and handle things" and by Thetan is meant "the spiritual being that is the basic self." An Operating Thetan, then, is one who can handle things without having to use a body of physical means.

OT Levels (sections, courses, etc.): the advanced Scientology training and auditing actions that enable a Clear to reach the state of Operating Thetan.

Overt: a harmful act or a transgression against the moral code of a group is called an "overt act" or an "overt". When a person does something that is contrary to the moral code he has agreed to, or when he omits to do something that he should have done per that moral code, he has committed an overt act. An overt act violates what was agreed upon. It is an act by the person or individual leading to the injury, reduction or degradation of

people into contact with Scientology and encourage their spiritual advancement through the higher levels of the religion. Missions minister basic Scientology religious services including the lower levels of auditing and introductory training.

Scientology Volunteer Minister (VM): Founded by L. Ron Hubbard in the early 1970s, the Volunteer Minister program was designed to provide practical Scientology tools and indiscriminate help in an often cynical and cruel world.

Scobee, Amy: Apostate of the Church of Scientology. Expelled. Admitted liar, caught sleeping with those she was counseling, dismissed from over 10 positions, couldn't meet the ethical standards of an average Scientologist, and Anti-Scientology Cult member.

Sea Organization, The (Sea Org): a religious order for the Scientology religion and is composed of the singularly most dedicated Scientologists—individuals who have committed their lives to the volunteer service of their religion. The Sea Organization is a fraternal religious order and is not incorporated. Members of the Sea Organization are therefore wholly responsible to the Church of Scientology to which they are assigned and are responsible, as are all other staff, to officers and directors of that Church.

Sheer: (adj.) Nothing other than; unmitigated (used for emphasis) (Oxford)

Slander: (n) The action or crime of making a false spoken statement damaging to a person's reputation. (Oxford)

Sleazy: (adj.) (of a person or situation) sordid, corrupt, or immoral.

(Oxford)

Sound Bite: (n) A short extract from a recorded interview or speech, chosen for its succinctness or concision. (Oxford)

Study Tech: the term given to the methods developed by L. Ron Hubbard that enable individuals to study effectively. It is an exact technology that anyone can use to learn a subject or to acquire a new skill. It provides an understanding of the fundamental principles of how to learn and gives precise ways to overcome the barriers and pitfalls one can encounter during study such as going by misunderstood words or symbols.

Suppressive Person (SP): a person who seeks to suppress other people in their vicinity. A Suppressive Person will goof up or vilify any effort to help anybody and particularly knife with violence anything calculated to make human beings more powerful or more intelligent.

Szasz, Dr. Thomas: American psychiatrist, university professor and writer, well known for his highly critical views of the practices of psychiatry. Szasz has written over 200 articles and several books.

Technology (tech): the methods of application of an art or science as opposed to mere knowledge of the science or art itself. In Scientology, the term technology refers to the methods of application of Scientology principles to improve the functions of the mind and rehabilitate the potentials of the spirit, developed by L. Ron Hubbard.

Thetan(s): the person himself - not his body or his name, the physical universe, his mind, or anything else; that which is aware of being aware; the identity which is the individual.

The Way to Happiness (TWTH): L. Ron Hubbard's The Way to Happiness is a common sense guide to better living comprised of 21 precepts, each predicated on the fact that survival is interdependent and without universal brotherhood there is no joy and there is no happiness.

Transgress: (v) Go beyond the limits of (what is morally, socially, or legally acceptable) (Oxford)

Travolta, John: Scientologist. John Joseph Travolta is an American singer, actor, and dancer. Travolta rose to fame during the 1970s, appearing on the television series *Welcome Back, Kotter* and starring in the box office successes *Saturday Night Fever* and *Grease*. (Wikipedia)

Unadulterated: (adj.) Not mixed or diluted with any different or extra elements; complete and absolute. (Oxford)

Unincorporated: (adj.) (of a company or other organization) not formed into a legal corporation.

Usher: (v) Cause or mark the start of something new.

Withhold: an unspoken, unannounced transgression against a moral code by which the person is bound is called a "withhold". A withhold is an overt act that a person committed that he or she is not talking about. It is something a person believes that if revealed will endanger his self-preservation. Any withhold comes after an overt.

Wright, Lawrence: A failed author and journalist that makes his living off projections and religious bigotry. He convinces, once credible, organizations to pay him money to attack new religions especially Scientology and its Founder.

Youth for Human Rights International (YHRI): a nonprofit organization founded in 2001 by Dr. Mary Shuttleworth, an educator born and raised in apartheid South Africa, where she witnessed firsthand the devastating effects of discrimination and the lack of basic human rights.

BUY AND READ THE
EXPOSING CRIMES SERIES BY
RYAN PRESCOTT ON AMAZON
AND THROUGH
EXPOSINGCRIMES.COM!

Printed in Great Britain
by Amazon